RUNIC
LORE AND LEGEND

"The magical runes of England have, ironically, been the most neglected of all the runic alphabets in writings in the English language. To have one of the leading authors on the wisdom of the runes pen this comprehensive manual on the Northumbrian wyrdstaves is a most valuable gift to all who follow the Northern Tradition. Pennick's weaving of local history and lore around the runes illuminates his subject in a way that no other book has been able to achieve."

RICHARD RUDGLEY, AUTHOR OF *THE RETURN OF ODIN: THE MODERN RENAISSANCE OF PAGAN IMAGINATION*

"Nigel Pennick is a true initiate who can demonstrate to the reader how nature and cosmos correlate to each other. He explains runes, medieval traditions, and Celtic magic in a pedagogic way that helps us understand how these topics are universal—something that gives us knowledge about ourselves and is of highest relevance for humankind today. I regularly return to Nigel Pennick's books and am delighted to add *Runic Lore and Legend: Wyrdstaves of Old Northumbria* to my shelf."

THOMAS KARLSSON, PH.D., FOUNDER OF THE ESOTERIC ORDER DRAGON ROUGE AND AUTHOR OF *NIGHTSIDE OF THE RUNES*

RUNIC
LORE AND LEGEND

Wyrdstaves of
Old Northumbria

NIGEL PENNICK

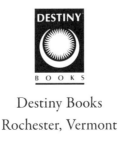

Destiny Books
Rochester, Vermont

Destiny Books
One Park Street
Rochester, Vermont 05767
www.DestinyBooks.com

Destiny Books is a division of Inner Traditions International

Library of Congress Cataloging-in-Publication Data

Names: Pennick, Nigel, author.
Title: Runic lore and legend : wyrdstaves of old Northumbria / Nigel Pennick.
Other titles: Wyrdstaves of the North.
Description: Rochester, Vermont : Destiny Books, [2019] | "Originally published in the United Kingdom in 2010 by Lear Books under the title Wyrdstaves of the North"—T.p. | Includes bibliographical references and index.
Identifiers: LCCN 2018025227 (print) | LCCN 2018038643 (ebook) | ISBN 9781620557563 (pbk.) | ISBN 9781620557570 (ebook)
Subjects: LCSH: Magic, Anglo-Saxon. | Runes—Northumbria (Kingdom) | Anglo-Saxons—Religion. | Folklore—England—Northumbia (Region) | Legends—England—Northumbia (Region)
Classification: LCC BF1622.A53 P46 2019 (print) | LCC BF1622.A53 (ebook) | DDC 133.4—dc23
LC record available at https://lccn.loc.gov/2018025227

Printed and bound in the United States by Versa Press, Inc.

10 9 8 7 6 5 4 3 2 1

Text design by Virginia Scott Bowman and layout by Debbie Glogover
This book was typeset in Garamond Premier Pro with Andea, Njord, Hypatia Sans Pro, PT Sans, Gill Sans MT Pro, and Avenir LT Std used as display fonts

To send correspondence to the author of this book, mail a first-class letter to the author c/o Inner Traditions • Bear & Company, One Park Street, Rochester, VT 05767, and we will forward the communication.

CONTENTS

INTRODUCTION

OUR PICTURE OF PAST TIMES

THE TECHNIQUES OF HISTORY AND FOLKLORE, including the study of the runes, often look at events and artifacts as if they were isolated phenomena with no context from which they emerged. Historical events are often seen as individual facts, and the surrounding physical, social, political, religious, and economic conditions of the time are scarcely taken in to account. Because of this, history becomes a broad picture of a sequence of more or less chaotic events, largely composed of war, conquest, oppression, enslavement, and sudden catastrophic change. Similarly, artifacts that come down to us more or less intact are here because for various reasons they have not been destroyed. Our picture of past times is thus a glimpse of near-random fragments. But from even such fragmentary and almost random records of events, often written down as propaganda for the winning or ruling group, it is possible to discern certain themes that are embedded in the fabric of tradition.

What is ignored by historians in the vast majority of cases is the place that magic has in history. Beliefs and techniques, like those inherent in the handicrafts, can be detected within those fragments we possess. An Anglo-Saxon sword, for example, is the result of more than one and a half thousand years of weapon-smithing using iron. It did not come into existence without incorporating all the knowledge gained by

1

Illuminated runes

experiment and experience over that time and the traditions—practical, social, and magical—practiced by the smiths themselves. Similarly, a historical account of an event from any year contains within it all the traditions and beliefs then current, whether or not the agents in the event were conscious of them. There are also overt instances of recorded magic. Through these embedded fragments we can discern the traditions and beliefs' continuity through changes in dynasties, regimes, and religions: what changed and what remained essentially the same.

This book is about the region of Great Britain known as Old Northumbria. In the early Anglo-Saxon period it was a kingdom in its own right. The physical geography of this part of Great Britain has, of course, scarcely changed in one and a half thousand years. But the political and ethnic boundaries *have,* time and again. History is a process of constant change; the ethnicities and boundaries of this region have altered an almost bewildering number of times in recorded history. This is certainly the case in the formative years of Northumbria: a long and complex tale of constant change, immigration, warfare, conquest, ethnic mixing, and the emergence of new identities. The Northumbrian runes, unique because they contain elements from all the cultures of the region, came into existence as the result of the emergence of these new identities. Magic also runs as a thread through this history.

Legendary history was the standard way of recording events in former times. Supernatural and magical intervention in human activities is the keynote of the adventures of the ancient Israelites recounted in the Bible. And it is the same in all cultures; each has the tendency to view itself as specially chosen, blessed by some power or deity that somehow marks that family, clan, tribe, race, religion, or nation as in some way better than all the others. Such a literal belief in one's exclusive specialness closes one's eyes to the fact that the others too believe this about themselves. But going beyond special pleading for godly decrees that specially chooses our group as superior to everyone else, we may learn a lot from this legendary worldview.

Legendary history tells us something about the interaction between humans living in the visible, material world and their relationship to the otherworldly, eldritch realm. In the Northumbrian context it is the Northern Tradition worldview that underlies its legends and history and that is embedded in the Northumbrian runes. This is explicit and implicit in all things done and produced there. Its spiritual heritage is implicit in all of its ensouled culture, having as its basis both a knowledge of and a practice of true principles. Here in the region of Old Northumbria immanence and presence coexist in an integrated tradition without being reduced to an image or a spectacle. If we bring ourselves into contact with this current, it will enable us to bring a symbolic reality into being. It is a reality that has been here as long as anyone knows, located in this particular region. By understanding it we may continually re-create the eternal in the present. This tradition is alive and available now, a fount of creativity for today.

1

THE KINGDOM OF NORTHUMBRIA

A Brief History

IT IS NECESSARY TO GIVE A BRIEF OUTLINE of Northumbrian history before and during the period when the Northumbrian runes came into being. Relatively little is recorded, for the region suffered repeated warfare for more than a thousand years after the fall of the Roman Empire. So much of the history is the recounting of battles, conquests, and reconquests of territory. The province called Britannia—much of the island of Great Britain—was part of the Roman Empire from the year 43 CE until about 410. After the rebellion of the Celtic queen Boudicca in 60 or 61 CE, the imperial territory was relatively stable, with occasional economic downturns, until the end of the third century, when a Roman admiral seized power and declared independence from Rome. The island was then reconquered by imperial forces with great destruction and loss of life. Increasing incursions were mounted by raiders from outside the empire: Picts and Britons from north of Hadrian's Wall, Scots from Ireland, and Germanic pirates. Some soldiers of the Roman army serving then on Hadrian's Wall were also Germanic men from Frisia.

The territory now called Scotland was not Scotland then, because the land of Caledonia was inhibited by three and then four distinct ethnic groupings or nations, each with its own language, just as Britain south of there was not yet England. The Picts, first mentioned in Roman writings in the year 297, appear to have been a group of tribes who spoke a form of the Celtic language. Their kings inherited their position through the female line. Whatever they called themselves, their name refers to their practice of tattooing themselves in honor of the gods and possibly of painting their faces and bodies at times of celebration and of war.

When the Roman Empire disintegrated at the beginning of the fifth century, various parts of Britain were invaded from different directions. The Scots were Gaelic-speaking people who, ruling in the north of Ireland, expanded eastward across the Irish Sea in to northern Britain and eventually, from about the year 500, became established there and eventually formed the predominant ethnicity in what became Scotland. Irish settlers invaded parts of Wales and lived there for several hundred years until they were exterminated by resurgent Welsh kings. Members of different Germanic nations came across the North Sea and settled more permanently in what became England.

In addition to all the ethnic changes, the ancestral religions of

Fig. 1.1. Portpatrick slate

these peoples were being targeted by enthusiasts for the Christian religion, which was the only official religion of the Roman Empire, though in Britain many of the pagan shrines continued to function until the empire collapsed. From the fifth to the seventh centuries Christian missionaries built up a network of monasteries from which they attempted to convert the local kings, lords, and chiefs. The early chroniclers of this time were all Christian clergymen and viewed the essentially chaotic events as a struggle between the pagan religions and Christianity. They saw history in terms of the inevitable spread of their religion and the downfall of those who would not accept their religious teachings. Hence the Christian parts of the history of this place in these times are far better documented than those of their opponents. So, for instance, we know a lot about King Pabo Post Prydain, whose shrine is at Llanpabo in Anglesey, because he was not only a Christian king but also became a monk in the later part of his life. Pabo had the epithet "the Pillar of Britain." He was one of what the old Welsh chroniclers called "the Men of the North," driven from his country, in what is now Scotland, by expansionist Picts in the early sixth century. He settled as a refugee in Wales and was buried at Llanerchymedd, near to Llanpabo, which bears his name. The Picts at that time were pagan, so the Welsh chroniclers presented an essentially ethnic struggle as a religious one between Christians and pagans.

Northumbria was founded by pagans from Angeln, the territory to the south of Denmark in the area now called Schleswig-Holstein. Northumbria was a double kingdom, composed of two distinct areas whose boundaries were defined by major rivers. The southern area, called Deira, extended from the River Humber in the south to the River Tees in the north. The northern area, called Bernicia, reached from the River Tees in the south to the Firth of Forth in the north. Northumbria was founded when Bernicia was settled by the Anglians, under their leader Ida, in the year 547. His son Ethelric built a strong-hold at Bamburgh on a steep rock on the coast about sixteen miles south of the present Berwick-upon-Tweed.

There was a long struggle for supremacy between the rulers of the two kingdoms and between them and the rulers of the neighboring kingdoms of Mercia, Cumbria, Strathclyde, Pictland, and Scotland. From about the year 600 the two monarchies of Bernicia and Deira composed a kind of federation of Northumbria. The north of the region was contested territory between the incoming Scots from Ireland and the Northumbrian Angles expanding northward. Indigenous to the territory were the British, divided into several kingdoms, and the Picts. Thus four ethnicities, speaking four different languages, were in conflict in what is now southern Scotland and northern England. Numerous battles ensued for control of the territory.

In the year 604, Northumbrian forces defeated the Scots of the Dál Riada at Degsastan, probably in Liddesdale. The British kingdom of Gododdin in Lothian was invaded and conquered by Northumbrian Angles in the late sixth and early seventh centuries. Æthelfrith, king of Bernicia, won a victory at Degsastan, invaded Deira, and expelled its king, thereby unifying Northumbria. In 617, Æthelfrith in turn was overthrown, and his three sons, Oswiu, Oswald, and Eanfrith, fled in to exile in Scotland and Pictland. King Edwin of Deira then expanded Northumbrian power up the east coast and established the town named after him—Edwinsborough (now known by its Scottish name, Edinburgh). Eanfrith, Æthelfrith's son, married a Pictish princess, and because among the Picts family descent was counted through the female line, subsequent kings of Northumbria had a legal claim on the throne of Pictland. In 632, Edwin was defeated in battle and killed by Penda, the pagan king of Mercia, whose army included forces of the king of Britain who were Celtic Christians. The magical elements leading up to this event are told in chapter 12.

Edwin was succeeded by Oswald, who was then slain in the Northumbrian-Mercian War at the Battle of Maserfield in 642. Oswald was subsequently succeeded by Oswiu, who extended the borders of Northumbria northward to the Firth of Forth, and Dunbar became a Northumbrian fortress. The expansion of Northumbria continued under Oswiu's son, King Ecgfrith. Under Ecgfrith, who reigned in the years 671 to 685, Northumbria pushed farther north in to the territory of the Picts, north of the Forth, around Stirling. The British kingdom of Rheged was destroyed at that time by a Northumbrian advance westward to the Solway. But the Northumbrians under Ecgfrith suffered a military defeat by Pictish forces led by Brude mac Bile in 685 at Nechtansmere, and the northern boundary of Northumbria was drawn at the River Forth. At its maximum in the north the Kingdom of Northumbria extended from the Solway Firth in the west to the Firth of Forth in the east. Farther north during the same period, Scottish expansion was overrunning the land of the Picts. At that time Northumbria stretched as far as Galloway, for an English cathedral was founded at Whithorn about the year 720. Kyle was occupied by the Northumbrians under Eadbert in 750 but was reoccupied by the kingdom of Strathclyde in 756. In that year, in alliance with Pictish forces, they overcame the Britons at Dumbarton Rock in the Firth of Clyde, which was a major citadel of the Strathclyde British.

The first Viking attacks on Britain were raids on Northumbria, when the monasteries of Lindisfarne and Jarrow were sacked in the years 793 and 794. These attacks ushered in the era of Viking expansion in the British Isles. The Vikings established themselves in Dublin in the year 841, when a member of the Norwegian aristocratic House of Vestfold, Olaf the White, declared himself king. Olaf soon extended his kingdom over Norse colonists who had settled in Galloway and the Hebrides. Ivar, Olaf's associate, was joint leader of the great army that invaded England in the year 865, conquering York and southeast Northumbria as far north as the River Tees and as far south as the River Humber in 867. Further incursions involved the submission of East Anglia, the execution of King Edmund in 869, and the invasion of Wessex in 871. Dumbarton was attacked again in the year 870, when it was besieged for four months by the "two kings of the Northmen," Ivar and Olaf, to whom it fell. Its surviving inhabitants were taken into slavery.

Northumbria rebelled against the Danes in 872 and 873, but their resistance was quelled. Halfdan, one of the Danish army's generals, gave up the war and settled his men—who had had enough of warfare—in Northumbria in 875. This serious depletion of the Danish fighting forces eventually led to the victory of the forces of Wessex under Alfred at Edington in May 878. Danish-held territory stabilized as the Danelaw about the year 880. The frontier ran broadly in a line from London in the southeast to Chester in the northwest. In the southeast the River Lea and the Great Ouse formed part of the frontier, while farther to the northwest from Passenham to Tamworth the border ran along the old Roman road called Watling Street. To the north of the line was the Danelaw, which in the east included present-day Essex, East Anglia, and Hertfordshire.

Scandinavian colonists arrived to settle in the occupied territories, including the Isle of Man, Cumbria, and what became Lancashire and the Wirral. In the north Northumbria became defined by the York-Dublin axis. These two cities were linked both directly by sea and by road in Great Britain, including the routes from the Wirral via Manchester and Leeds, across the Pennines through Ribblesdale and Wharfedale, by the old Roman road between York and Carlisle, by sea from Dublin up the Firth of Clyde, overland across lowland Scotland, and again by sea from the Firth of Forth to York.

Dumbarton Rock was plundered by the forces of Ragnall when, in the years 914 to 918, he sought without success to take control of the whole of Northumbria. Vikings from Ireland finally captured York in 919 and took over Deira. Early in the tenth century the British kingdom of Strathclyde was conquered by the Scots. Bernicia, the unoccupied Anglo-Saxon part of Northumbria, was invaded in the year 927 by Norse forces under Guthfrith. But Norse power was severely impaired by the forces of the king of England, Æthelstan, at the Battle of Brunanburgh ten years later, when a coalition army composed of Scots, Welsh, Norwegians, Danes, and Irish was decisively defeated. The last Scandinavian king of York was Eric Bloodaxe, slain in the year 954

Fig. 1.2. Image of the Celtic god York

in an ambush at Stainmore. Around the same time, Edwinsborough was finally conquered by the combined forces of King Malcolm II of the Scots and Owen the Bald, the last king of Strathclyde, who overcame the English of the Lothians at the Battle of Carham in 1018. The Northumbrian English were killed, enslaved, or driven out. King Malcolm also soon did away with the Welsh-speaking British in Strathclyde, thereby establishing the border of Scotland, which was extended southward by force of arms by King David I, as far as the Tees. Finally Scottish expansion was halted at the Battle of the Standard at Northallerton in 1138. The border between England and Scotland had stabilized around the present line by the early thirteenth century.

2

THE SPIRIT LANDSCAPE
OF NORTHUMBRIA

TRADITIONAL SPIRITUALITY IS ALWAYS BASED on the activities of everyday life. Climate and landscape give it its physical character; hunting and farming its deities, customs, and festivals. Traditional spirituality is intimately tied up with landscape, climate, and the cycle of the seasons. The same features of this region's landscape were sacred to all the different ethnic groups who lived there in former times: Picts, Britons, Romans, Angles, Scots, and Norse. Hills and mountains, springs, rivers and lakes, ravines and caves, special rocks, and trees each had their particular mark of veneration. Local people ritually ascended holy hills on the festal days of the sky gods. Offerings were cast into rivers, lakes, and springs at certain times of year as offerings to the indwelling spirits in thanksgiving or propitiation. Holy trees were protected by fences and decked with garlands and ribbons, and food was left for their indwelling dryads. Sacred signs, images of gods and animals, were carved on rocky outcrops; stopping places along tracks and roads were punctuated by shrines to local gods as places of devotion for travelers. In Northumbria local cults and shrines were honored by every ethnic group; the sacred places of the Celts were reconstructed under the Romans and honored by the Anglians. When the centrally organized Christian Church arrived, these places became shrines and churches of the new religion. Many of the customs and practices not directly connected with religion continued through all the changes as folk traditions.

Each place or landscape feature has its spirit guardian. European traditional religion is pluralistic and polytheistic. The landscape was filled with wild animals, some of which still exist in greatly diminished numbers and others that have been exterminated: aurochs, bears, wild boars, wolves, lynx, wolverines, wildcats, beavers, sea otters, many kinds of snakes and lizards, and vast flocks of birds. The spirits of the land were revered as the old gods, demigods, and sprites who oversaw the well-being of fields and flocks.

Certain places have their landwights, or earth spirits: they are crop, water, and tree sprites; spiritual protectors of travelers and seafarers; supernatural beasts who appeared unwanted, like trolls, water monsters, werewolves, dragons, and demons; personifications of disease and death; and malevolent demons, bringers of bad luck. They are the innate spiritual qualities of places, personified in terms of guardian spirits, giants, boggarts, fairies, elves, trolls, goddesses, and gods. Under the Romans these were systematized into the Roman pantheon, the Interpretatio Romana, where a Celtic war god like Cocidius was assimilated with Mars as Mars Cocidius, the syncretic linking of one god's function under the aegis of a similar Roman one. Later, before the arrival of Christianity, the Germanic gods fulfilled the same function, assimilating the local *numina* under new names. Then the incoming Christians syncretized many of the older Germanic and Celtic gods with their devil. Many centuries later the same process was at work. Travelers who reported having seen the traditional rituals of Northumbrian harvesttime likened the harvest queen with the goddess Ceres.

Ancestral holy places—homesteads, grave mounds, tombs, and battlefields—are held in veneration as special places of the ancestral spirits. Tales were and are told of particular events that took place there, which give their names to those places still. Gods, saints and devils, heroes and villains, *ostenta* and accidents, all have their places in placenames and their stories. Some are unchanged, as places where people can experience transcendent states of timeless consciousness, receive spiritual inspiration, and accept healing. Each of these various otherworldly beings is a human description of the innate eldritch qualities of places that the Romans conveniently characterized as the genius loci, the spirit of the place, to whom they erected altars and in whose honor they conducted rites and ceremonies.

Unlike the later Christian interpretation of spirituality, there was no distinct barrier between gods and lesser spiritual beings. The religions of the Pictish, Celtic, Germanic, and Nordic peoples were centered not so much on a chief deity as on the veneration of a divine ancestor. In early times the king's ancestor was also the tribal god, and this principle was maintained among the Angles and Saxons in England. Seven out of the eight Anglo-Saxon royal genealogies begin with Woden, as does the Swedish royal line. The runes, obtained by Woden's self-sacrifice,

Fig. 2.1. Woden

are integral with this tradition. The ancestors also played an important role in the everyday religion of the common people. An *idis* is a female ancestral spirit honored as a guardian of a clan, family, or individual. Folk-moots, the forerunner of parliaments, were held on moot hills. Many of these are the burial mounds of ancestors whose help was invoked in collective decision-making.

From the ninth century at the latest, labyrinths made of turf or stones were used in the rites of spring, for ceremonies for the dead, and weather magic. Local lore of labyrinths identifies them as dwelling places of fairies. The turf labyrinth at Asenby in Yorkshire is actually called Fairy Hill, where those who ran the maze could hear the fairies singing at the center. Early Christian churches were built on many sacred places such as these when the old religion was destroyed, though the spirit of what went before is still discernable at some places more than a thousand years later. Places that could not be appropriated by the church had their indwelling spirits redefined as legendary characters or hateful demons identified with the Christian devil. But despite the ostensible triumph of the Christian religion in England, successive kings felt it necessary to promulgate new laws against the practices of the Elder Faith. The Dooms of King Canute, who reigned from 1020 to 1023, were yet another attempt to ban indigenous traditional sacred practices. One of Canute's definitions was "Heathendom is . . . that they worship heathen gods, and the sun or moon, fire or rivers, water wells or stones, or forest trees of any kind."

The most complete literary record of the northern European sacred landscape is Icelandic. During the ninth and tenth centuries the uninhabited island of Iceland was colonized by settlers who came in the main from Norway and the Western Isles of Scotland and were predominantly pagan. Their religious response to the landscape is recorded in the text called *Landnámabók* (The Book of the Taking of the Land). These settlers were acutely aware of the spiritual nature of place. Certain areas were deemed inappropriate for human habitation. They were reserved for the *landvaettir,* "the landwights, the spirits of the

Fig. 2.2. Labyrinth at Dalby

place." The settlers performed ceremonies in honor of the landvaettir, and offerings were left for them. Pagan prayers were directed toward Helgafell, the holy mountain of Iceland, and before praying devotees washed their faces out of respect. These recorded accounts of Icelandic piety tell us a lot about the religious practices that existed in northern Britain before the imposition of the Christian religion as the only faith permitted by law.

The Northumbrian spiritual understanding of the land is directly related to the forms of the landscape, the climate, and the cycle of the seasons. The same features of landscape are sacred in the various indigenous ethnic traditions of Europe. They are hills and mountains, springs, rivers and lakes, special rocks, caves, and trees. Each has its particular marks of veneration, sacred times of "keeping up the day" when rites and ceremonies are conducted. Each has its spiritual correspondences with the beings and forces of the eldritch world, which, though usually unseen, are ever present. In acknowledgment, sacred signs, runes, and images of gods and animals were painted or carved on rocky outcrops where the spirit was perceived to be strong. Holy trees were protected by fences and bedecked with garlands and ribbons. Stopping places along tracks, drifts, and roads were marked by cairns, standing stones, rag bushes, posts, and shrines to local gods as places of devotion and thanksgiving for wayfarers. Nine Standards Rigg is such a Northumbrian holy high place, crowned by nine cairns. Mountains were climbed ritually on the holy days of the sky gods. Offerings were thrown ceremonially into lakes and springs at certain times of year in thanksgiving or propitiation.

Carrawbrough in Northumberland is the site of the Roman fort of Brocolitia. It contains a temple of Mithras and a holy well dedicated to the goddess Coventina. In imperial days the spring was inside a Celto-Roman temple. An image of the goddess reclining on a leaf and votive offerings, as well as nearly fourteen thousand coins, were found here. After the introduction of the Christian religion there were many attempts to ban the veneration of holy wells and their indwelling deities. For example, the Penitential of Archbishop Egbert, who reigned from the years 736 to 766, stated that people should be severely punished "if any exercise divinations and soothsayings or keep vigils at any spring or at any other creature, except at the Church of God." In principle these theocratic edicts were enforced, but in practice they could rarely be policed. So all except the most devout Christians took little notice of these and other religious laws, though many were punished and even killed for ignoring them if they got caught by the religious authorities.

It is clear that the substitution of a Christian deity for a pagan one just meant that the original pagan one was worshipped in the guise of the latter, as in the modern syncretic religions of the Caribbean and South America. The transference of older rites into a newer religion is inevitable. Holy wells bearing the names of Christian saints are an example of this substitution of name without altering the use. For example, Saint Baldred's Well at East Linton in East Lothian is supposed to commemorate a Northumbrian saint of the early eighth century, if Baldred is not actually a Christian reworking of the northern solar god Baldur himself. Lady's Well at Holystone, Rothbury, Northumberland, is a well whose location is said to have been discovered by an apparition of Our Lady. It was used by the missionaries Ninian and Paulinus to baptize people into the Christian religion. If it is indeed the result of an apparition of Our Lady, and was used by the Christian mission to Northumbria, it predates the first attested one, at Walsingham in Norfolk, which took place in the year 1060.

The sacred days of the pagan year are significant in the traditions at holy wells in old Northumbria. Many are associated with the rites of May. Lovers went at midnight on May Day to the Pin Well at Wooler, Northumberland, to throw in a bent pin, wishing to be brought together with their lover. Another May Day wishing well in former Northumbria is Saint Anthony's Well in Holyrood Park, Edinburgh. The Well of the Holy Rood is nearby. Our Lady's Wells at Longwitton in Northumberland are a group of three wells in an oak wood. One well has chalybeate waters, one aluminous, and one sulfurous. They were resorted to at midsummer and on the following Sunday, when the waters were taken, gingerbread sold and eaten, and traditional midsummer games played. Saint John's Well at Harpham in Humberside is the holy well of Saint John of Beverley, who was born at Harpham. A ritual is conducted there on the Thursday nearest to May 7, which is the saint's day. The water had the power to subdue wild animals. Saint Hilda's Well is in the churchyard at Hinderwell, North Yorkshire, eight miles from Whitby, and the tradition there is to make licorice water from it on Ascension Day.

Other wells bear the names of local clergymen, which may point to some rite they conducted to take them over from the Elder Faith. Saint Cuthbert's Well at Bellingham, Northumberland, is close to the church, and its water is used in baptisms. Another Saint Cuthbert's Well exists at Donington, near Albrighton in Shropshire. The water from this well is used for treating eye ailments. Saint Cedd's Well at Lastingham, North Yorkshire, is close to the shrine of Saint Cedd, where his bones were kept in a specially constructed crypt where they could be viewed by pilgrims. A holy well of Saint Chad is in the same village. Saint Oswald's

Well, Oswestry, Shropshire, though not within the boundaries of the kingdom of Northumbria, is significant in the mythos of King Oswald, who was killed nearby at the Battle of Maserfield in the year 642. Within the boundaries of the kingdom is another Saint Oswald's Well, at Kirkoswald in Cumbria. Mother Shipton, the medieval seeress (1488–1561), is associated with the Dropping Well at Knaresborough in Yorkshire. All over the British Isles, holy wells were kept by hereditary guardians. The divinely enthused *derilans,* who kept the holy wells of Scotland, and the wisewomen of England and Wales ministered to any passing pilgrim who sought an oracle or the boon of healing.

In traditional societies travelers perform rites and ceremonies before setting out and during their journeys. Certain trackways, called *yries*— "pagan trackways"—in ancient texts, had their ways and stopping places marked by rags, shoes, and specially planted trees. Aspen trees (*Populus tremula*), with their characteristic white leaves, were planted to mark boundaries, and in later times Scots pines (*Pinus sylvestris*) were planted to denote stances on the routes taken by drovers driving their herds southward from Scotland to East Anglia or London. As a visible marker for the drovers, who were navigating across the country without maps, the pine recalls its runic meaning. Wayfarers said prayers and made offerings at sacred stopping places along these tracks, droves, and drifts. The Cheese Well on Minch Moor, two miles southeast of Traquair in the Borders Region, was a stopping place on the cattle drovers' road, at which wayfarers were accustomed to deposit a piece of cheese in the water as an offering. Fords were particularly hazardous places. They were marked by shrines and also messages of practical help for those on the road. A Pictish stone at Borthwick Mains in the Borders has a carving of a fish on it. This stone once stood in a ford in the River Teviot as a depth mark. When the river level was above the flat edge of the fish's tail it indicated that the water was too deep and therefore too dangerous to ford.

Crossroads are places of transition, where the axis linking the underworld with the upperworld intersects this world on which we walk. As with all liminal places, it is a place of physical and spiritual dangers. Here the distinction between the physical and nonmaterial worlds appears uncertain, and the chance of encountering something otherworldly is more likely than at other places. When the Roman Empire ruled this region crossroads were acknowledged with a *herm,* an image of the god of traffic and trade, Mercury. This godly image, which indicated the right road and guided the traveler's footsteps, was the generalization of the particular spirit of each individual crossroads. Later, Christians erected stone crosses where pagans' stones or sacred trees stood. The Northumbrian monk Ovin from Lastingham is one who did this. Gallows were set up at crossroads for the execution of criminals, and until 1823 the bodies of the executed, suicides, and non-Christian people such as wisewomen and Romani were often buried at the crossroads.

Out on the fells cairns were erected at places where sacrifices took place or where a wayfarer had died. The rune Stan signifies such places. Cairns can be seen silhouetted against the horizon, markers for travelers across the fells. On Dunmail Raise, the pass linking Steel Fell and Seat Sandal between Ambleside and Keswick in Cumbria, is a notable cairn. It commemorates a battle between the forces of the Scottish kings Duvenald and Edwin. Before the battle each Scot laid a stone on the pile; afterward each survivor took one away. Those that remained served as a receptacle for the spirits of the dead, commemorating and numbering the slain, creating a sacred place to be honored in hero and ancestor worship. At one point in history the cairn marked the border between England and Scotland, and later, when the Scots border had changed once more, the line between Cumberland and Westmorland. It was a sacred act of remembrance to place a stone on it with a prayer. Today flowers are left by the roadside where one has died accidentally. Cairns occupy liminal areas of decision: decisive battles, which are places of transition in history; mountain passes, decisive places of traveling from one valley to the next; and borders between territories, decisive places of tribes or nations. On the fells cairns are spiritual way stations that commemorate those who have passed before, both travelers in this world and the dead.

Some landscape legends are magical interpretations of historical events. Dumbarton, from the Scots Gaelic name Dunbreatan, meaning the fort of the Britons, which at one time was in Northumbria, appears as a stronghold of the Elder Faith. The story tells us that in the year 388 the pagan faithful there rebelled against the activities of the Christian missionary Patrick, who was attempting to impose his religion there as he later did in Ireland. Patrick was expelled and left for Ireland in a curragh. The Rock of Dumbarton, a much-contested military stronghold that dominates the southern shore of the Clyde estuary, is said to have been thrown there by the pagans who attempted to sink Saint Patrick's vessel. Another version of the story says that the rock was thrown at Patrick by the devil. Near the hill called Yeavering Bell, where the royal temple of pagan Northumbria stood, is a standing stone called the Druid's Lapful. It has this name from a legend in which a woman Druid was once carrying it in her apron, but the apron string broke and it fell to Earth, where it remains.

At Melrose Abbey is the grave slab of the thirteenth-century wiseman Michael Scot, reconstructed from nine fragments. He is said to have made a brass head that could talk and to have built a road across Locher Moss in one night. It's more certain that Scot's book, the *Introductions,* was the first European book of practical astrology. The legend of Lord Soulis tells how Thomas the Rhymer discovered how to bind the evil baron in one of Michael Scot's grimoires. Beneath Scot's tomb is said to be an ever-burning lamp that wards off the spirits of the night. In the borderlands are certain stones called witchstones or weirdstones. Most witchstones in Scotland are boulders set up to mark the place where a witch was burned during the particularly virulent Scottish witch hunts of the seventeenth century. Unlike in England, where supposed witches were hanged, in Scotland they were burned at the stake. The prehistoric earthwork of Doon Hill, east of Dunbar, is notorious as a place of witch burnings.

Putting up a stone to commemorate the place of the judicial murder was a later version of the pagan tradition of building a cairn at the place where someone had died. Indeed at Doon Hill the number of stones in the cairn is the number of people killed there as witches, like the number of slain warriors on Dunmail Raise. At Spott, not far away, is a witchstone that commemorates another burning. At Auchencrow, in the Borders Region in former Northumbria, is a witchstone of a different kind. The Peg Tode Stone is built into a retaining wall at the western end of the village's main street. Local legend asserts that this stone was carried there from Coldingham by a witch. On passing the stone one must say, "Peg Tode, Peg Tode, don't touch me."

Islands are inherently special places, protected by a water barrier from unwanted physical and psychic influences. Many islands, ranging in size from small offshore rocks, islets, and eyots in rivers to large islands such as Man and Anglesey, were held in reverence as holy islands. In pagan northern Europe there were several of the smaller islands dedicated as shrines. Islands are under the protection of specific deities whose shrines there maintain the sacred integrity of the place. In the Baltic Sea the island of Rügen and in the North Sea both Heligoland and Walcheren are notable sacred places. The deities Rugevit, Forseti, and Nehalennia, respectively, were present on these islands, where they were attended by dedicated priesthoods who conducted their worship and, in some cases, corps of men-at-arms sworn to protect them.

Certain smaller islands were also deemed sacred to specific deities, and it was on them that unofficial non-Christian guardians continued to revere the sacred places well into the nineteenth century. Islands allow people who live there to adopt modes of living that are separate from the everyday world of the mainland. Spiritually they can be viewed as eldritch places, the undying lands, the otherworldly abodes of the dead. For the living they have supported hermitages, monasteries, and spiritual communes. Their isolation makes them separate realms politically as well as spiritually, so in the Celtic tradition they often stood alone as independent territories. An early Christian monastery in Northumbria was founded by Celtic monks at Lindisfarne on Holy Island. The wooded island of Saint Herbert, south of Keswick in Cumbria, was a retreat of a kind better known in Celtic Christianity. But Saint Herbert was not a Celt, as his name clearly shows. The holy island of Dunholme is where Durham Cathedral stands as the shrine of Saint Cuthbert, whose bones were carried from place to place before being deposited there as the result of divination.

PAGAN CONTINUITY

A few days' sailing from ostensibly Christianized early medieval Northumbria were places where the pagan religion was flourishing. In Saxony was a shrine with a very tall pole they called Irminsul, "the universal pillar." It was destroyed by the forces of the Holy Roman Emperor Charlemagne in the year 772 during his crusade against the Saxons. The shrines of the god Forseti on the holy island of Heligoland, which were easily accessible from English east coast ports, were destroyed in the year 785. But when Northumbria was taken over by Viking adventurers, whichever of the pagan customs, rites, and ceremonies had not been suppressed by the church were reinvigorated by this new influx of heathen practitioners. In the Viking age of Northumbria major temples of the Nordic gods stood at Jellinge in Denmark; Sigtuna and Gamla

Fig. 2.3. Irminsul

Uppsala in Sweden; Mæri, Lade, Skiringssal, Trondenes, and Vatnsdal in Norway; Kialarnes in Iceland; and Dublin in Ireland.

Sweden was officially pagan until the year 1100, and paganism continued to flourish even later farther east. The land of Pomerania, now divided between Poland and Germany, had several major pagan temples, many on islands in navigable rivers. They were destroyed by Christian fanatics between 1124 and 1128. Also in the Baltic was the holy island of Rügen with its temples, the largest of which was dedicated to the god Svantovit. This was destroyed in a Christian crusade by Danish forces in 1169. So, until Northumbria was wasted by the Normans, there was always direct contact with ancestral religion in mainland Europe and Scandinavia within a few days by ship from the east coast ports.

In any case, there is a wealth of evidence that the traditional understanding of sacred places was not destroyed by the Christian religion, only absorbed and modified. For example, Saint Wilfred built Hexham Abbey using stones taken from Roman remains. The crypt has a passage in which is part of a Roman altar dedicated to Apollo Maponos, and the font is fashioned from part of a pillar from the pagan temple. Saint Wilfred's Church at Cantley, Doncaster, is on another place where once a Romano-British temple stood. Being syncretic, the church absorbed the practices that were not obviously at odds with official doctrine and gave them new interpretations in line with orthodoxy. So many elements of the Northern Tradition continued in a scarcely changed form, as in the use of traditional holy locations and the veneration of luck-flags.

3
NORTHUMBRIAN GEOMANCY

The Year, Time, and Space

THE EIGHT AIRTS

We are so used to counting in tens, using decimal coinage and metric measurements, that it is difficult sometimes to think in other ways. The traditional way of dividing things is not in tens, for this "one size fits all" approach of modern commerce is not the natural way of doing things. The basic way to divide things is to cut them in half, then in half again, and so on. This means of division is thus twofold, fourfold, eightfold, sixteenfold, and so on. Traditional weights and measures as well as time were based on an eightfold system, and contemporary paganism divides the yearly cycle by eight major festivals. The compass rose is the most widespread example today of the division of space by the repeated halving method, having thirty-two basic divisions. This is derived from our natural perception of the world we see around us. In agricultural and seagoing societies people are always aware of the horizon, which is visible from where they are—both for the observation of the apparent motions of the sun, moon, and stars and to be in harmony with the powers inherent in the shape of the landscape.

In old Northumbria the basic layout of the land was visualized according to natural measure by the division of the circle into its four quarters by conceptual lines running north to south and east to west. Between these lines the horizon was divided by additional lines running to the intercardinal directions. This created the eightfold division necessary if one is building a square or rectangular building or an enclosure facing the four quarters of the heavens. The southern quarter is the quadrant between southwest and southeast; the eastern quarter is between southeast and northeast; the northern sector is between the northeast and the northwest; and finally, the western quadrant is between the northwest and the southwest. The four cardinal directions are thus at the midpoints of the four quarters. In the region of old Northumbria these eight directions are called the *airts,* and across the Pennines they are called *haevers.* The Roman landscape engineers in Britain, members of the guild of *agrimensores,* had used a related system, the sixteenfold Disciplina Etrusca, for laying out temples, fortresses, and cities. This was a particular skill that embodied Etruscan spiritual principles, divination, and augury. How far it was known outside expert circles is uncertain.

Because of the considerable differences in day length during the year in northern Europe, the awareness of the directions was more highly developed and widespread there than in many other parts of the world, for it was a necessary part of survival. The knowledge of the airts was an integral part of the knowledge of farmers, builders, seafarers, wisewomen, and cunning men. This awareness of directions has subtle ramifications in all manner of areas, unsuspected by those who have never encountered a traditional landscape.

These eight directions come from the physical structure of the planet we live on: the north-south polar axis and the east-west one at right angles to it, the plane of the Earth's rotation. These are the fixed directions inherent in our planet's structure. But in addition to these physical directions there are variable directions defined by the apparent motions of the heavenly bodies in relation to the fixed ones. These have a cyclic nature. Depending on our latitude, the visible position of the rising and setting sun at the solstices (the longest and shortest days) and at other celebrated times of the year will be at different places on the horizon from the intercardinal directions. Furthermore, the height

Fig. 3.1. Runes and airts

of the horizon above or below our viewing point will alter the rising place of the sun, moon, and stars. And unless the site has an equal-height horizon all around it, we will not see the celestial bodies rising and setting symmetrically with relation to the cardinal directions. On a level horizon there is an annual solar geometry where the midsummer solstice sunrise is diametrically opposite the midwinter sunset, and the winter solstice sunrise is directly opposite the midsummer sunset.

How long daylight lasts varies with the season. Northumbria is between the latitudes 53°40' and 56°, so the difference between day length at midwinter and midsummer is considerable. The range between the height of the sun at noon on midwinter and noon on midsummer is also notable. Between the southernmost rising of the sun at midwinter and the most southerly sunrise at midsummer, the sun rises due east at the equinoxes, crossing the east-west line southward in winter and northward in summer. This defines the two halves of the year, the dark half and the light half. Between the two solstices the traditional rural calendar marked the end and beginning of winter at the festivals of May Day, or Beltane, and All Saints' Day, or Samhain, respectively, May 1 and November 1 in the modern calendar. In the traditional rural landscapes of the past, viewed from farmsteads or sacred places, these rising, setting, and standing points were indicated either by natural features or by artificial markers such as standing stones, specially planted trees, or cairns. These are known by their Norse names of *dagsmark* and *eyktmark*. Where natural features mark these important days, it is clear that the location from which they are viewed was chosen with regard to the airts related to the natural configuration of the horizon. This may be seen admirably at many stone circles in this region, whose location attests to the high level of knowledge of their constructors.

In addition to the location of sunrise at notable times of year, these markers also indicate the time of day when the sun stands over them. When the sun rises due east at the equinoxes it is 6:00 a.m. in the modern clock reckoning of time, and when it sets due west it is 6:00 p.m. When the sun stands due south at any time of year it is

Fig. 3.2. The sun in the trees casting long shadows

12:00 noon, but the sun at midsummer stands much higher in the sky, the highest it will ever reach at that latitude, than at noon on the winter solstice, when it is at its lowest point. In his work on Northern Tradition astronomy and time-telling, Otto Sigfrid Reuter noted,

"Among all peoples the time of day has been told by the position of the Sun, Moon, or stars above fixed landmarks such as mountains, trees, and other high spots on the horizon." At any time of year when the sun is above the horizon it will always be above the same horizon marker at the same time of day.

The word *day* is used to denote two different things. The period of daylight between sunrise and sunset is called day, as opposed to night. But a day is also the period defined now as twenty-four hours. These two different systems caused confusion when the Christian religion was introduced. The Christian division of time was developed by the early monks in Egypt to govern the times of their daily prayer cycle. Their "temporal hour" system of time-telling divided the day of daylight into twelve equal hours. There was not a serious difference between the length of the day in summer and winter at about 30° latitude. But in Northumbria, 36° farther north than Egypt, the length difference between summer days and winter days *is* serious. In *Skylore of the North,* Otto Sigfrid Reuter wrote, "Since the nights in winter are longer than the days, but in summer shorter, the daylight hours are unequal: the daylight hours are shorter in winter than in summer. In Mediterranean latitudes the difference was acceptable; in Iceland, however, where the day (from sunrise to sunset) lasted twenty-one of our hours in summer but only three hours in winter, the corresponding hours by the church's method had the length in summer of one and three-quarters hours and in winter of a quarter of an hour by our modern reckoning. The uselessness of the medieval 'Temporal Hour' system inevitably roused resistance soon after its introduction into the North, having led to great confusion there."

In the octaval system of northern Europe the tides of the day are not related to the length of daylight but rather to a whole cycle of light and dark. There are eight equal divisions called tides for the modern twenty-four-hour period, reckoned as beginning and ending at 7:30 a.m. in modern reckoning. These tides are not related to the tides that ebb and flow in the sea. The markers of the tides are always the same, so sunrise and sunset vary between the tides. In winter a certain point in a tide will be in darkness, while in summer at the same point it will be light.

In Northumbria there remain a number of sundials marked for the traditional northern time-telling tides. Kirkdale Priory in North Yorkshire has a sundial using this system. It dates from between the years 1056 and 1066. Carved next to it is Old English text that translated reads, "This is the day's sun-marker at every tide." Other inscriptions record the makers Hawarth and Brand, who were priests, and Orm, son of Gamal, who reconstructed the church after it had fallen into ruins. At Escombe, Durham, dating from the second half of the seventh century, is another tidal dial. Others exist at Old Byland and Weaverthorpe in Yorkshire and one at Edston, with an inscription telling us that it is the time-teller of travelers. A dial divided for the tides of the day and the twelve-hour system is carved on the stone cross at Bewcastle, dating from around the year 675. It is an interesting survival from an age of dual systems of time-telling.

The eight tides of the day as observed in old Northumbria, described in the twenty-four-hour clock system, are

Morgan, from 4:30 a.m. to 7:30 a.m.
Daeg-Mael, 7:30 a.m. to 10:30 a.m. This is the first tide of the day.
Mid-Daeg, 10:30 a.m. to 1:30 p.m.
Ofanverthr Dagr, 1:30 p.m. to 4:30 p.m.
Mid-Aften, 4:30 p.m. to 7:30 p.m.
Ondverth Nott, 7:30 p.m. to 9:30 p.m.
Mid-Niht, 9:30 p.m. to 1:30 a.m.
Ofanverth Nott, 1:30 a.m. to 4:30 a.m.

The directions played an integral part in traditional ways of life. The traditional reckoning of solar time was used in northern Europe until the arrival of cheap clocks and the imposition of standardized time, first by railway companies, then by governments.

SEASONS OF THE
OLD NORTHUMBRIAN YEAR

The monastic chroniclers hated the rites and ceremonies of the pagan countrypeople around them: in their fervent faith they felt it was essential to obliterate local ancestral traditions and impose the Christian religion on the pagans. Yet in their attempts to discredit the Elder Faith, they wrote enough to preserve the knowledge of what our spiritual ancestors did, so that we can understand the meaning of their rites and ceremonies. Bede tells us that the ancient Angles divided the year into two halves, defined by the solstices. The halves are subdivided by the cycles of the moon into six months each. Each solstice is guarded by two months. In the winter there is Ærra Geola, before Yule, the month before the winter solstice; and Æftera Geola, after Yule, the month after it. In the summer two months bracket the summer solstice: Ærra Liða comes before midsummer and Æftera Liða after it.

Paralleling the Anglo-Saxon months with the modern names, January is Æftera Geola, February is Sol-monaþ (mud month, later called February fill-dyke), and April is Eostre-monaþ, which was reckoned as the first month of spring. Eostre is the Anglo-Saxon goddess of the dawn and of the springtime, and she gives her name to the festival of Easter, though the date of the latter is reckoned according to a modified version of the ancient Jewish calculation of Passover. May is called Þri-milce—three milkings, the month of such abundance that the cows produce freely.

Ærra Liða is equivalent to the modern month of June, while July is Æftera Liða. August is Weodmonaþ, Weed Month, and September is Halig-monaþ, Holy Month, the month in which the pagan harvest festival was celebrated. The name was finally banned, and the new month name Hærfest-monaþ, Harvest Month, was substituted for it. The beginning of winter was with the month called Wynterfylleþ, our October. November is Blot-monaþ, Sacrifice Month, when the farmers who were slaughtering livestock that could not be overwintered dedicated them as sacrifices to the gods. Excavations at the Northumbrian temple site at Yeavering found a large pile of the bones and skulls of oxen inside the east door of the temple. Next to the temple was a smaller building, probably a cookhouse. The animals killed and dedicated to the gods were served up in the royal hall nearby. Finally, December is equivalent to Ærra Geola.

THE HALYMAN'S RIG

Just as time measurement integrates the cycles of the day and the year with sacred times, so sacred places play a significant part in northern spirituality. All over northern Europe there is the custom of fencing off pieces of ground as holy, deliberately set aside from everyday use. These pieces of land are not churchyards or graveyards but rather eldritch places. They are well-known in the Borders Region and Scotland, where pieces of fenced ground are called the Goodman's Field, the Halyman's Rig, the Gudeman's Croft, the Black Faulie, or Clootie's Croft. These are places where neither spade nor plow is permitted to touch. Typically they are a triangular corner of a field, fenced and dedicated by the smallholder or farmer with a promise never to till the earth there. Within the boundary the pristine condition of the earth prior to cultivation is preserved. They are places where the landwights can exist undisturbed.

In addition to triangles at the corners of fields, uncultivated triangles of grass at the junctions of roads are called No Man's Land, denoting their nonhuman ownership. Elder trees (*Sambucus nigra*) often grow in the Halyman's Rig, and veneration of this tree was specifically prohibited as a "heathendom" by a law of King Edgar (reigned 959–975 CE). Later folk tradition states that each elder tree is inhabited by a sprite called Lady Ellhorn, otherwise known only by the epithets the Old Girl or the Old Lady. Other early Christian laws forbidding heathen customs in England, Norway, and Sweden that forbade people from worshipping at groves, stones, and in pagan sanctuaries also designated the places called Stafgarðr, land fenced with posts. Their triangular form is overt in the Norse sacred enclosure called the *vé*. These are characteristically triangular enclosures, fenced off from the everyday world by a row of uninscribed stones called *bautasteinar* or a fence called the *vébond*. Very large examples of this sanctuary form exist—long, narrow V-shaped enclosures with the sacred places aligned along the middle line. Jellinge in Denmark is the most notable, with royal burial mounds and a temple where the cathedral now stands on the centerline. York too has a sacred layout, which may be recognized as a vé, where churches stand in alignment on its centerline.

According to ancient law judicial combats or duels had to be conducted formally in place, magically separated from the everyday world. They took place either on an island, in a special enclosure such as a circle of stones, or on a hide pinned to the ground by *tjosnur,* ritual pegs with heads. Hazel wands were used as shooting marks in northern English archery, as attested by the legend of William of Cloudesly. In Anglo-Saxon England temporary enclosures for judicial single combat and even full-scale battles were delineated from the everyday world by a fence of hazel posts erected by the heralds in charge of the proceedings, by the rite of enhazeling ground. The decisive Battle of Brunanburgh, fought in the year 937, was on an enhazelled field. There English forces led by King Æthelstan under the banner of Saint John of Beverley routed a much larger Confederation army composed of Scottish, Welsh, Irish, Danish, and Norwegian units.

The veneration of the triangular corner is maintained to this day in central Europe in the shape of the Herrgottswinkel or Heilige Hinterecke (Lord God's Corner or Holy Back Corner), a house shrine high up in the corner of the main room overlooking the family table. Largely maintained in Roman Catholic households, its corner position relates it to the Halyman's Rig and the dwelling place of the house spirits in the pagan tradition. In the countryside of Northumbria the hidden heritage of fenced enclosures, No Man's Land and the Halyman's Rig, attest to an unbroken continuity of venerable age that continues today.

Other holy places with no particular natural features are marked traditionally by standing stones, single posts, images, sacred pavilions, and temples. The *wih* was a sacred image standing in the open. More substantial was a shrine covered with a tent or pavilion, the *træf,* "a rocky outcrop." Places called Trafford recall shrines by river fords. In Scandinavia and Scandinavian colonies communal worship took place in the *hof,* an ordinary hall-form farmhouse, which had a special extension, the *afhús,* where sacred objects and images were kept. Here regular festivals to mark the passing of the seasons were observed. The ceremonial enclosure at Yeavering was the largest of such complexes in Old Northumbria, with a temple, sacred posts, ancillary buildings, and a royal hall where sacrificial feasts were held on festal days. These holy places, surrounded by sacred boundaries, were places where sacred law ruled and everyday behavior had to be tempered by respect for the presence of the gods. Weapons were not allowed in the sacred places, for they desecrated the sacred peace of the pagan temples, and this principle continued once the Christian religion took over, for the Law of the Northumbrian Priests forbade any priest from taking weapons into the church. Thus churches, which were declared sanctuaries, continued an older pagan tradition.

The greatest sanctuary in northern England is the collegiate church of Saint John the Evangelist at Beverley. This was a place where lawbreakers could claim sanctuary from the enforcers of the law. In the year 937, after his victory in the Battle of Brunanburgh, King Æthelstan returned to Beverley to return the banner of Saint John, which had protected his army. There he gave the minster a royal charter: "In your church shall be founded a college of canons, endowed with ample possessions. It shall be a sanctuary, with a *Friðstool* before the altar, as a place of refuge and safety for debtors and criminals. Four stones, each a mile distant from this place, shall mark the bounds of the privileged ground. Your monastery shall be extended, and revenues increased, and the shrine of the Blessed John shall be amongst the most magnificent in the land."

The sanctuary of Beverley extended for a mile and a half around the minster. It had six levels. Outside the church there were two boundaries, an outer and an inner. The outer boundary line was called the *leuga*. (The later *baneluca* around Bury St Edmunds in Suffolk is in the tradition of the Beverley sanctuary.) The crossing points into the areas of the sanctuary and between them were marked by standing-stone crosses. The third boundary began at the churchyard, the fourth at the nave door, the fifth at the choir screen, and the sixth level was the *friðstool* (a sacred seat of peace) itself. Violation of the sanctuary was punished by progressively larger fines, depending on the place within the hierarchy of sanctity the offense occurred. The least fine, in the outer area, was one hundredth, £8, and inside the second boundary the fine was doubled. If sanctuary was violated in the choir the fine was £144. If a fugitive wrongdoer had reached the friðstool and was seized, the person seizing was deemed bootless, an outlaw whom it was every law-abiding person's duty to kill.

Any fugitive from the law who gained the sanctuary, including people who had escaped from jail, was permitted to stay there for thirty days, while the canons made legal representations for a pardon. The fugitive was given accommodation and food within the precincts of the minster. When the period of grace was up, if there was no pardon, the fugitive, carrying a cross, was taken to one of the crosses on the other limits, where he met a coroner. Either he was arrested and tried, or, if he swore an oath abjuring the realm, he could go into exile in another country. The coroner stipulated the miscreant's journey to a particular port, the road taken, the authorized stopping places, and the number of days in which the journey must be completed. If the miscreant did not follow the prescribed route he was deemed an outlaw and subject to beheading. The alternative to abjuring the realm and going into exile was to forfeit one's possessions to the crown and taking an oath of obedience to the minster and town. Then he became a frithman who could never leave the bounds of Beverley but was allowed to attempt to make a living there through his trade. Ripon Cathedral and Hexham Abbey each also have a friðstool, but neither place had the full-blown system of sanctuary that existed at Beverley. The right of sanctuary was abolished in England in 1623.

THE YORK CORRIDOR OF SANCTITY

In the city of York is an alignment of seven sacred places now called the Corridor of Sanctity. It is a line, which is aligned almost north-south, bisecting the city between the Rivers Foss and Ouse. The confluence of the rivers is the apex of the vé, at a place called Saint George's Field. The line first runs through the site of a chapel that belonged to the Knights Templar and was dedicated to Saint George. Beyond this is the defensive Clifford's Tower, containing an eleventh-century chapel. North of this along the line is the Church of Saint Mary Castlegate, also dating from the eleventh century. Farther along the line is the municipal church, All Saints' Pavement, a church whose foundation dates, like the minster north of it, which is also located on the line, to the seventh century. Between All Saints' and the minster is Saint Samson's Church, dedicated to an early sixth-century Welsh saint who was reputed to have been an archbishop of York. North of the minster the line crosses the chapel of the Archbishop's Palace. Thus there are seven sacred buildings on the axis of this river-defined vé. The central line links them all in a spiritual axis just as the fundamental stave is the focus on which the runes are formed.

4

RUNES AND CONSCIOUSNESS

Weaving the Web of Wyrd

THE NORTHERN TRADITION, which was the worldview of the people who founded Northumbria, sees human existence as part of a worldwide fabric of people, things, and events traditionally called the Web of Wyrd. The Old English word *wyrd* is derived from the verb *weorðan*, which means "to become" or "to come to pass." It is cognate with the Latin verb *vertere,* "to turn." We talk about how events have turned out, and *wyrd* means "an individual's fate, position in the world, or destiny." But this Northern Tradition concept does not mean that life is predestined, an idea that is present in the contemporary usage of the word *destiny.* Here the warp of the woven fabric of the Web of Wyrd is seen as time and events, while the weft is composed of individual human acts. As the process of weaving the web continues, the pattern of interactions of the threads, which are lives and events, irreversibly comes together. So it was that in Old English, a historian is called a *wyrdwritere.* The notion of our fate as being woven by Wyrd is evident in the Old English saying *"me thet wyrd gewaef"* ("Wyrd wove me that," i.e., "that is my lot in life"). The Old English word *gewaef* or *gewif* also means "fortune or destiny." Wyrd is something that cannot be altered or undone: *wêwurt,* "woeful Wyrd," is inevitable and invincible. Even the gods are subject to Wyrd, in both the Northern Tradition and English Christianity. As an Old English gnomic verse in one of the Cottonian manuscripts tells us, "The glories of Christ are great: Wyrd is strongest of all."

Icons of the goddess Frigg, Queen of Heaven, portray her with a distaff and spindle, or riding on a distaff in the manner of a witch on a broomstick. A twelfth-century mural in the Cathedral of Schleswig in northern Germany, the ancestral land of the Angles, shows her thus. Northern Tradition astronomy calls the starry heavens Frigg's Cloak. The spindle with which she spins is the North Star, Polaris, while her distaff is marked by the three stars called the Belt of Orion in Graeco-Arabic astronomy. This image of the divine spinner is reflected in Christian images of the annunciation, which depict Mary spinning with a spindle and, beside her, a woven wickerwork basket containing wool. A Northumbrian example is a ninth-century stone panel at Hoveningham in North Yorkshire. Although connected with the story of Jesus, the weaving of destiny by the woman who enables new human life to come into the world does not originate in Judaeo-Christian tradition. It is present in Greek and Roman cosmology, where three sisters representing the past, the present, and the future are shown participating in the three stages of weaving. The first spins the thread from the raw materials. The second weaves the various threads spun by the first into a fabric, and the third cuts or rips the fabric apart. In England these are the Weird Sisters, and the fabric woven by the middle one is the Web of Wyrd.

Telling of the Weird Sisters, whom the Norse call the Nornir, the Icelandic poem *Voluspá* recounts that the "staves did cut, laws did they make, lives did they choose: for the children of men they marked their fates." The Nornir have a name that is interpreted as "those who speak," being related to the Middle English verb *nurnen,* "to say." Their utterances or decrees are expressed in the language of runic writing as the Old English words *stafir* and *stafas,* "staves." Staves can mean both runic characters and the wooden staves on which they are cut, runestaves cut on a runestaff. The runes are integral with fate and record: the Old English word *wyrdstafas* refers to the decrees of fate, and *endestafas* is death. But whatever happens to us is the result of how we act within the conditions we find ourselves, for we have free will within our circumstances. The Northumbrian saying "Let us dree our Wyrd" expresses this reality. We are within the given circumstances and must endure their difficulties, but how we endure them and how we deal with our circumstances is up to us. Fate works in accordance with nature; all things that come to individuals are neither rewards nor punishments sent by the gods, but they are the inevitable consequences of actions. Thus we all meet our *metod,* our destiny, doom, and death.

The runes are fundamental to understanding something of the weavings of the Web of Wyrd. At the present day the common view concerning alphabets, other than taking writing and reading for granted, is that they are solely practical in character. They are considered as functional necessities that are required for written communication and the conduct of everyday life. The possibility that there may exist within them some deeper significance rarely emerges into commonplace awareness. But if we begin to penetrate beneath appearances, we enter the realm of many concepts and connections that demonstrate the basic unity of life that is the Web of Wyrd. For in the use of characters to represent sounds and numbers, we penetrate the mysteries that lie at the foundations of existence. Unfortunately the concept of a stave is not taught to children in school, for there the utilitarian ethos rules regardless of the type or denomination of school.

Alphabets are derived from pictograms and glyphs that stand for actual things or actions as well as phonetic sounds. The modern Western alphabets, including Hebrew, Greek, Roman, Cyrillic, and Arabic, owe their source to an ancient Canaanite script, which developed into two major versions, Phoenican and Aramaic. Alphabets to the east of Syria were derived from the Aramaic, while those to the west, from the Phoenician. Hence the ancient alphabets of Europe, including Etruscan, Oscan, the various forms of Runic, Gothic, Church Slavonic,

Fig. 4.1. Wyrdstaves of the North

the Aibítir of Gaelic, and the Coelbren y Beirdd of Wales are all derived ultimately from the Phoenician script of three thousand years ago.

The runes have a special place in the European Tradition. The alphabetic glyphs that we call runes are what appear in the mind when the word *rune* is heard. But a rune is not just a letter of an alphabet; it also can be a song, an incantation, or an invocation as well as a glyph pregnant with symbolic meaning either as an alphabetic letter, an idogram, or a symbol—in some cases all at the same time. So a rune is more than just a letter in an ancient alphabet. The actual meaning of *raunen,* in Old English *run* and in Middle Welsh *rhinm,* was "mystery." This meaning tells us that within the simple figure, composed of a few lines, lies a great deal more than its surface appearance. Fundamentally a rune is a mystery, a secret, and by *secret* is meant something that is more than just an unknown meaning for a person who is illiterate. Each stave that we call a rune is a unit of embedded lore, a storehouse of knowledge and meaning. As a symbol a rune represents a formless and eternal reality that is rooted in the world as we experience it.

Many of the runestaves began in ancient days as pictographic symbols, written down a long time before they became a means of communicating any specific message between people. The use of these signs as an alphabetic script came later. Prerunic symbols known as the rune hoard exist in ancient European rock art, which includes ideographic signs and sigils, which possessed meanings that we can make good guesses at because we know the meaning of the same signs from later contexts. These were not incorporated into the later rune rows. These include sacred glyphs, calendar symbols, and devices, covering the entire storehouse of preliterate Germanic and Celtic rites and religions.

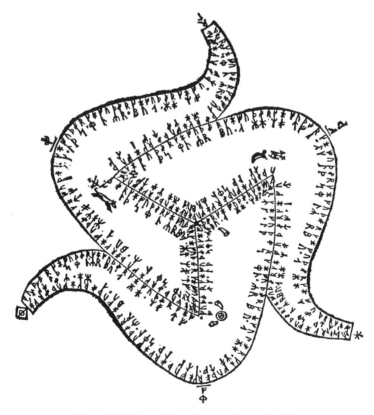

Fig. 4.2. Scandinavian runic calendar

These signs, sigils, and symbols have their earliest authenticated dates in the Hällristningar, carvings of the late Bronze Age and the transition to the Iron Age (circa 1300–800 BCE). About two thousand years ago some of these symbols were taken up and identified with certain characters from the Etruscan alphabet from southern Europe, and a new phonetic alphabet was born: the Futhark. This act of creative genius is recorded for us in *The Edda,* where it was through Odin, master of magic, poetry, and inspiration, that this synthesis, or rather, realization, took place. In the song *Hávamál—The Utterances of the High One,* stanzas 138 and 139 read:

> *I know that I hung on the windswept tree,*
> *Through nine days and nine nights,*
> *I was stuck with a spear*
> *And given to Odin,*
> *Myself to myself*
> *On that tree, which no man knows*
> *From which roots it rises.*
> *They helped me neither by bread,*
> *Nor drinking horn.*
> *I took up the runes,*
> *Screaming. I took them,*
> *Then I fell back from there.*

Hávamál exhorts in the next verses: "Hidden runes shalt thou seek, and interpreted signs; many symbols of might and power by the great Singer painted, by the High Powers fashioned, graved by the Utterer of the gods." This ancient account of a shamanic experience—terrible and life changing—is recognizable to any who have undergone such a terrifying ordeal, willingly or by accident. The psychic trauma, close to death, dismembers the old persona, and if the individual survives he or she is reconstructed in a subtly different manner. Odin, known as Woden in the English tradition, received the knowledge of the runes through a shamanic revelation, as a shaman riding out of the body through the nine worlds of northern symbology, passing through the complete cycle of time as symbolized by nine days and nights, nine being the number of completion.

This number is at the root of northern cosmology, being found in traditional measures, rune lore, and in cosmically significant board games such as Tablut and Nine Men's Morris. As three times three, its form squares the threefold, or triadic, nature of the runes. This three-fold structure is in the form, symbolic content, and numerical value of each rune: taken as a totality they describe the complete structure and function of all that is and can be: the process of coming into being and the nature of that being. Shamanism gives access to eldritch areas of being that can rarely be reached in everyday states of consciousness. Thus the runes, grounded in the eldritch, mediate between the various realms of understanding, description, and the unspeakable inner work-ings of the mind and the cosmos.

The symbolism of the tormented flash of shamanic insight, which enabled Odin to release the full potential of the runes for the benefit of humankind, describes a moment in history when the two sides of the brain were linked by response to a single sign. Modern research into the difference between the right and the left hemispheres of the human brain has shown that it is the left side that is used for the skills of writ-ing and reading. In the Northern Tradition worldview the interconnec-tions of nerve pathways in the brain are an aspect of the Web of Wyrd. The alphabet, and the Futhark in its phonetic use, symbolizes a fully phonetic representation of language in a qualitatively different man-ner from that of ideographic or other nonphonetic systems of linguistic notation. Physical injuries to the left side of the brain in persons using alphabet-dominated linguistic systems are associated with impairment or loss of writing and reading skills.

The transition of the runes from the ancient rune hoard, where each character was nonalphabetic and nonphonetic, to the alphabet sys-tem may be interpreted as a changeover in the use of the sides of the brain from right to left. Studies on the abilities of either side of the brain by various researchers have shown that the hemispheric representation of nonalphabetic writing systems differs markedly from that in alphabetic ones. Logographic characters, such as Egyptian hieroglyphs or the symbols used on runestocks or clog almanacs, are more efficiently recognized by the right side of the brain. The nonphonetic *kanji* writing in Japanese, for example, is processed by different areas of the brain than is *kana,* the phonetic system used alongside kanji. People who suffer from brain damage in different areas can understand either one or the other system, depending on the location of the injury.

The representation of nonphonetic hieroglyphs in the right side of the brain in opposition to the left may even be superior to the use of the left side for the phonetic system, for the person may interpret them directly without the interposition of phonetic decoding. If prealphabetic systems of writing were decoded by the right hemisphere of the brain, then the differences between the nonphonetic and phonetic systems may be more fundamental than hitherto recognized. The right hemisphere is associated with the intuitive, creative abilities, rather than the left hemisphere's analytical, linguistic function. In the runic system, in its predecessor in the rune hoard as well as in its late manifestation as the calendric runestock or clog almanac, one can trace the continued use of the right side of the brain when dealing with the concepts associated with space, time, and their representation as the runes. Investigation of the runes, and their late flowering as runestocks, must take this qualitative difference in to account, for it produces a qualitative difference in the perception of the world from the traditional and the modern viewpoints.

European traditional spirituality never dismisses matter as an illusion; neither is it considered to be "fallen" and thus less real than the spirit; nor does it view matter materialistically as dead stuff, devoid of creative potential. The natural cosmos may be viewed symbolically as constituting the materialized body of the Divine Principle, for it embodies fundamental structural and dispositional axioms that manifest themselves continually as discernable elements of the physical world. These can reveal themselves spontaneously or may be identified by human intelligence. Traditional spirituality recognizes them as divine principles that operate throughout the cosmos, from the smallest to the largest. In this sense the visible can be interpreted as an emanation of the invisible. These true principles can be seen as the signature of divinity.

When we work with these true principles we attempt to use our skills to bring the external forms of matter into harmony with them. We recognize these simple truths and work with them. The sublime infinite may be grasped by attuning ourselves with certain inexpressible aspects of the Web of Wyrd. These are, in a real way, to us at least, symbolic presentations of the infinite, unveiling to us hitherto unrealized parts of our existence. At such places and moments the distinction between the self and the external other loses its significance. The difference between subject and object falls away in oneness.

5

THE RUNES OF NORTHUMBRIA

On the horn's face were there
All the kinds of letters
Cut right and reddened.
How should I read them rightly?

THE ANCIENT LAY OF GUDRUN

THE MAJORITY OF WRITINGS about the runes deal with the twenty-four-character rune set known as the Common Germanic Futhark among academics and the Elder Futhark among runemasters and diviners. This is taken as the fundamental rune row, called Futhark from the first six characters—*F, U, Th, A, R, K*—because it is wrong to call it an alphabet as it does not commence with *A, B* (*alpha, beta*). The runes as an alphabet came into existence more than two thousand years ago in the Alpine region now called the Tyrol. But the oldest complete rune row is carved on an early fifth-century standing stone at Kylver on the island of Gotland in the Baltic Sea. Other early examples are known from finds in the present-day countries of Bosnia-Herzegovina, Sweden, France, Germany, and the Netherlands.

The runes are metaphors of reality, exploring the presence of the infinite within the finite. At their most basic the runes refer to one or another of the elements of the inner structure of existence. The runes' names come from everyday things, characteristics, and processes. In addition to the literal meaning of a rune as, say, a birch tree, the meaning goes deeper than the mundane level. Each rune encompasses all of the connections, ideas, and correspondences that link to it. So each rune is a storehouse of knowledge and meaning.

As they traveled, new runes entered the rune row. In Friesland the row expanded to twenty-eight characters sometime about the year 600. The Anglo-Saxon Futhork is a development of this, with twenty-nine staves. Coins of sixth-century kings of East Anglia and Mercia bear these runes. The oldest text, which gives the meaning of each rune, is *The Old English Rune Poem.* Dating from the eleventh century, it contains elements dating as far back as the eighth century. Frequently writers on the runes use the reconstructed hypothetical Old German names of the runes (e.g., *Thurisaz, *Ansuz, *Teiwaz, but without the asterisk that denotes that the word is not actually recorded in ancient texts). Working with names that may or may not be those used by the ancient runemasters is fraught with difficulty. In this book, the names of the runes are the original Old English ones.

About the year 800 in England, north of the River Humber, Northumbrian runemasters of Anglian descent added a further four runes to the Anglo-Saxon rune row, making thirty-three. The Elder Futhark is divided conventionally into three airts, groupings of eight runes, so the Northumbrian rune row is divided into four airts, often called by their Old Norse name, *aettir* (singular, *aett*). The fourth is known as "the airt of the Gods." In addition, the thirty-third rune, Gar, is seen as a central point around which the four groups of eight are circled. Some of these additional Northumbrian runes have Celtic influence, being related to the Ogham alphabet of the Irish and British bards.

In many places the Anglians of northern England and the indigenous Celts lived together in peace and cooperation. There was intermarriage between the Northumbrian and Pictish nobility. And among

Fig. 5.1. Runic bract,
twentieth century

the artisan class there was cooperation and interchange between the different ethnic groups. For example, the Mote of Mark, in Dalbeattie Forest, Kircudbright, Scotland, had a mixed Anglian-Celtic population. It was a center of excellence of metalworkers. A rune-inscribed bone was found there in excavations during 1973. The history of Northumbria is a story of continual contact between the different ethnic groups in the region. Because the incoming Angles were living in an area whose predominant culture was what is called Celtic today, Celtic elements are part of the Northumbrian runic repertoire. The illuminated artwork of surviving texts such as *The Lindisfarne Gospels,* made by Eadfrith near the end of the seventh century, is in a style that amalgamates typically Germanic animal styles with Celtic designs known from comparable work in Ireland.

Pictish, Irish, and Scottish priests were instrumental in bringing the Christian religion to prominence among the Northumbrians. But, just as in Anglo-Saxon England, where the heathen tradition continued in parallel with Christianity, the Celtic Church had earlier incorporated pre-Christian Druidic concepts into its practices, if not its teachings. This included the Ogham tree alphabet, where each letter is named for a tree, a bird, or some other thing that is emblematic of the quality of the letter. Runic codes used in Northumbria and the Nordic realms, such as *hahalruna,* worked on the same principle as the Ogham characters, where numbers of strokes related to a stave denoted the letters.

The fact that runes were used on Christian memorial stones and crosses shows that they were valued in Old Northumbria and not abandoned at the changeover of religions. In 1833 a number of small gravestones with names in runes were discovered at the early Northumbrian monastic graveyard at Hartlepool. They have crosses on them, but their form is the same as pagan runic memorial stones of the same age. Others are known from Lindisfarne. These were not unofficial runestones; the shrine of Saint Cuthbert of the year 698 at Durham had a runic inscription. An eighth-century cross fragment from Lancaster now in the British Museum has runes asking the reader to pray for Cynibalþ Cuþber, and another, much longer text exists on the cross at

Fig. 5.2. Stone cross fragment with runes, Hackness

Bewcastle in Cumbria. This cross is thought to be a memorial to King Oswiu's son Alcfrith.

The church at Thornhill, near Dewsbury in Yorkshire, yielded three cross fragments with runes, including some binding runes, dating from about the year 800. Two very smashed fragments of the same period at Hackness exist with unencrypted and cryptic runes. In the eighth century a stone cross eighteen feet tall was set up at Ruthwell in Dumfries, which is now part of Scotland but was then part of Northumbria. It was smashed as an "idolatrous monument" by order of the Assembly of the Scottish Church in 1642, but in 1801 the fragments were brought together again, though one part is missing. Its inscription uses thirty-one Northumbrian runes in a text of the Christian poem *The Dream of the Rood.* The runes here include two that are unique and one from the Scandinavian Younger Futhark. From these surviving inscriptions, other runic artifacts, and several manuscripts that somehow were not destroyed, and of course, the three rune poems—*Old English Rune Poem, Norwegian Rune Poem,* and *Icelandic Rune Poem*—are all explanatory poems that give the meaning of each rune in poetic form. Thus the runes were preserved and so were their meanings, both secular and magical.

The knowledge and use of the runes is unbroken since their inception. They were in everyday use in Sweden as writing until the late seventeenth century; they were used in secret by wisewomen and cunning men; and they were used to count the days of the Julian calendar on wooden almanacs until that calendar was superseded by the Gregorian. Thus runic almanacs were used in Estonia until 1921. Also scholars have always studied the runes, along with antiquarians and archaeologists who have collected and documented rare and choice artifacts. The runes used today are predominantly from the Elder Futhark, as the system has been popularized in divination from about 1960 onward. But each system of runes has its advantages in different contexts. The Northumbrian runes are specific to an area of Great Britain and so are of especial interest to esotericists and pagans who live there.

6

THE FIRST AIRT
OF THE
NORTHUMBRIAN RUNES

ᚠ

FEOH-WEALTH

The Northumbrian Futhork, like the Elder Futhark, commences with Feoh. This is the primary rune of the first airt and whose meaning is "cattle." Before the supremacy of money as a measure of value, traditional societies measured their wealth in heads of cattle. So the first characters of the Hebrew, Greek, and Gothic alphabets also mean "cattle." The cow plays an important part in the Northern Tradition creation myth, which tells of the Primal Cow, Audhumla, who licks a crystalline block of salt from which comes Buri, the father of the human race. Symbolically Feoh is thus the primal origin of us all, while prosaically it represents movable wealth. In contemporary terms Feoh refers to money: a fee, a payment.

Figuratively Feoh is the power to gain worldly success and great wealth, and to keep it. Magically the rune is used in workings for power and control. It is invoked to supply the power to begin a working, drawing in all of the energy we need to start up and keep going. But, as with all workings of rune magic, we must take account of the implications of what we do. We must be responsible for our actions. This is stressed in the reading for this rune in two of the ancient rune poems. *The Old English Rune Poem* says, "Wealth is a comfort to everyone. But he who wishes to cast his lot for judgment before the Lord must share it." And *The Norwegian Rune Poem* tells us that wealth can easily lead to greed and envy, which bring the downfall of society: "Wealth causes friction between relatives, while the wolf lurks in the woods." Feoh's herb is the stinging nettle (*Urtica dioica*). Its tree is one of the most magically powerful, the elder (*Sambucus nigra*).

ᚢ

UR–AUROCHS

The second rune is called Ur. It represents the great European wild ox called an aurochs (*Bos primigenius*), which once was widespread in northern and central Europe. Unfortunately the species is no more. It was impossible to tame or train the aurochs, so it was hunted to extinction. The aurochs was killed off in Britain about 1300 when King Edward I ordered the extermination of all wolves, aurochs, and foxes. The legend of Guy of Warwick killing the monstrous Dun Cow probably refers to an aurochs. The first two species on King Edward's list were totaled, but the fox escaped because the lords enjoyed hunting them and did not want to put an end to their sport. Gradually hunting eliminated the aurochs from other European lands, and the last aurochs of all was shot in 1627 in Poland. In addition to its formidable bulk and power, the aurochs was noted for its long, sharp, curving horns. *The Old English Rune Poem* describes its characteristics: "The aurochs is bold with horns rising high, a fierce hornfighter who stamps across the moors, a striking animal!" Because of their immense length and capacity, aurochs horns were used as ceremonial drinking horns. The traditional Scottish ceremonial drinking cup, the corn, is an aurochs horn with a lip of chased silver. A fine example was used until the early twentieth century at Dunvegan Castle in Scotland. Anyone who drinks from an aurochs' horn partakes of some of the *maegen* (personal force) of this noble beast.

Although the species has been killed off, the runic power of Ur is still available. Magically Ur is a channel for the tameless might of the Primal Ox. It brings the runemaster into direct connection with the boundless power of the universe. Above all others, Ur is the rune for power, stamina, and perseverance. Overall it is one of the most empowering runes, providing the basic energy for all magical workings that require a solid grounding. Thus it is used to anchor a working in a specific way or at a particular place. Because it emanates from a tameless, therefore collective, power, Ur can never be used selfishly. Ur cannot be owned by or controlled by an individual. Workings using Ur can only be according to free will, for the good of all. So although the power of Ur can bring personal success, it will not be to the detriment of others. The magical herb of the Ur rune is the lichen called Iceland moss (*Cetraria islandica*). Ur's magical tree is the silver birch (*Betula pendula*).

ᚦ

THORN-THORN

The third rune is Thorn, and it is primarily a rune of the thunder god Thunor (Thor) and the power of giants. On the twig the thorns protect the plant. They function passively, deterring attackers, who injure themselves if they grasp the thorns. *The Old English Rune Poem* tells us, "The thorn is very sharp, an evil thing to grasp, very grim for anyone who rests among them." This rune signifies the power of resistance present in thorn trees and the power of the earth giants known as Thurs and Moldthurs. Hence Thorn embodies the power of defense. Thorn is thus the divine power that resists everything threatening us. It is thus a magical protection. Just like

Thunor's lightning, magically the Thorn rune can produce a sudden change without warning. Used effectively it can significantly turn the course of events in another direction. Thorn is especially powerful at places in the landscape sacred to Thunor, places with names such as Thundersley, Thorley, Thorney, Thornton, Thornbury, Thornhill, and so forth. This principle should not be ignored: the geomantic awareness of people in the past still remains potent in place-names that describe specific local qualities.

Thorn's corresponding trees are the blackthorn (*Prunus spinosa*); the May tree, or hawthorn (*Crataegus monogyna*); the bramble (*Rubus fruticosa*); and the oak (*Quercus robur*). Thorn's corresponding herb is the houseleek (*Sempervivum tectorum*). When grown on the roof this is a traditional protection of the building against lightning, the weapon of Thunor. In this aspect Thorn represents the willful direction of the generative principle, the masculine creative energy in action. As the letter *þ* it is still used in the everyday Icelandic alphabet.

OS—MOUTH

Os is the fourth rune of the Northumbrian rune row, though in the twenty-nine-character Anglo-Saxon rune row it is the twenty-sixth. It is the rune of Woden in his aspect as god of eloquence and linguistic communication. Os is literally the mouth from which the divine sound of creation emanates. On a cosmic level this signifies the primal vibrational note that empowers material existence. Magically Os denotes the creative power of the word and, hence, by extension, divine and human wisdom. More generally it refers to information, whose expression on a physical level underlies the very processes of life itself. Os reaches to the basic level of human culture, which is expressed in poetry, song, saga, and literature. When it is used in magic it is at its most powerful when connected with call spells known as *galdr*. It serves to bring the divine breath, *önd,* into action. Os is allied to the ash tree (*Fraxinus excelsior*), and its herb is the hallucinogenic fungus the fly agaric mushroom (*Amanita muscaria*), used historically by wisewomen and shamans.

ᚱ

RAD—RIDING

The fifth rune is Rad. This is a very important rune, representing ritual and process. The name Rad means "wheel" and, by extension, "the motion that the wheel allows, traveling or riding." In magical terms Rad signifies the vehicle that we can use to achieve an objective, but, just as a wheeled vehicle cannot be used without a road on which to run, Rad also represents the road or process itself. Rad is thus both the way forward and the means to get there. Magically Rad is primarily a rune of command and control, for it allows energies to be channeled and transformed. Rad empowers the transfer of spirit, matter, or information from one place to another. We can use it to channel magical energies in an appropriate way, according to our will, to produce the results we require. But to take full advantage of Rad's power we must be in the right place at the right time, and, of course, we must be doing the right thing. An important use of Rad is as a facilitator of personal transformation, for it helps us to take conscious control of our Wyrd. Rad's associated element is air. It has a male polarity. This rune's trees are the oak (*Quercus robur*) and the wayfaring tree (*Viburnum lantana*), while its corresponding herb is mugwort (*Artemisia vulgaris*).

ᚲ

CEN—TORCH

The sixth Northumbrian rune is called Cen. It signifies a flaming torch made of the resinous wood of the pine tree. The northern

English and Scots dialect word *ken,* "knowledge, illumination," is the general meaning of this rune. Thus Cen is a rune of teaching and learning, bringing clarity in understanding, just as a burning brand brings light to a dark place. Cen is therefore a rune that connects the runemaster with the mystery of transformation. This is achieved through the union and transmutation of two separate entities into a third, which did not exist before the operation. Cen can take a number of forms, depending from which rune row it comes. Its most common forms are < and, alternatively, *a*.

It is written as a branch arising from a straight stave. In this form it signifies the active principle. It is the polar opposite of the eleventh rune, Is, whose single stroke signifies the static principle. This upright form is the shape of the ancient northern European lamp, a floor-standing vertical holder supporting a fiery chip of pinewood, burned for lighting. *The Old English Rune Poem* expresses this with, "The torch is living fire, bright and shining. Most often, it burns where noble people are at rest indoors."

Because Cen brings us light in the outer darkness, symbolically it brings the inner light of knowledge. As the fire of the hearth, Cen represents the power of the forge in which material is transmuted by the smith's will and skill into something new and useful. The disordered raw materials of nature are put into order by human consciousness using the powers inherent in nature. Magically Cen is used in workings concerned with personal illumination or involving acts of creativity. Cen can be used to channel protective energy and regenerative powers and to empower all positive actions. It has the corresponding trees of pine (*Pinus sylvestris*) and bilberry (*Vaccinium myrtillus*). Pines were planted as markers on the routes taken by cattle drovers, showing stances where cattle could be pastured overnight. This is fully in keeping with its runic meaning. And the cattle connection is present in Cen's herb, cowslip (*Primula veris*).

GYFU–GIVING

The seventh Northumbrian rune is Gyfu, which means "gift." The ancient mark of sanctity is *X,* the linking rune that symbolizes connections between people or the gods. As the gift, Gyfu is the act of unification through exchange. It denotes the oneness of the donor and the person to whom the gift is given. *The Old English Rune Poem* expresses this, "To men, giving is an ornament displaying worth, and to each outsider with nothing else is yet substance and honor." The key feature of Gyfu is to bring balance. The Northern Tradition personifies this through the goddess Gefn, whose title is the "Bountiful Giver." Magically Gyfu provides access to powers that link us with other people or the human level with the divine. This rune is useful in magic that involves interchange between people, such as cooperation between two individuals. This may be to further a common cause or a business partnership. When used magically this rune should not be written as a crossing of two lines, but as the combination of two strokes, > and <, touching each other at the apex. When they are written horizontally they represent a connection between two people on an equal basis. But when written one above the other these strokes signify the connection between the human, living on Earth, and other powers, either above in the upperworld or below in the underworld. As a glyph this rune is called the pagan cross, a mark of consecration of holy places and objects. In other contexts it is often called Saint Andrew's cross, though often the name is used in contexts where there is no reference to the saint. This rune is heraldically a saltire, the glyph of the flag of Scotland, whose patron is Saint Andrew. Whether this has its origin in the runes or in church symbolism is questionable. Gyfu's element is air, and it has no polarity. The corresponding trees of the Gyfu rune are the ash (*Fraxinus excelsior*) and the wych elm (*Ulmus glabra*). Its herb is the wild pansy, or heartsease (*Viola tricolor*).

ᚹ

WYN–JOY

The last rune of the first airt is called Wyn. Its shape represents a metal weathervane or a fabric flag, which, though fixed on a staff, moves according to the changing winds. Wyn thus signifies joy, that elusive state of harmony within a chaotic world. Magically we find joy by coming into balance with events, just like the weathervane, remaining centered yet accommodating change. This rune is thus the midpoint between opposites. It removes alienation and anxiety, whether they are caused either by shortage or by excess. Wyn is a rune of fellowship, shared aims, and general well-being. Magically this rune assists us in the realization of our true nature. Once we are centered in our proper shape then we can use the rune to fulfill our needs. Wyn does this by leading us toward harmonious ways of doing things, thereby transforming our life for the better. Wyn manifests itself in Northumbrian tradition through the luck-flags that were instrumental in military victories. The Wyn rune's tree is the ash (*Fraxinus excelsior*), and its corresponding herb is flax (*Linum usitatissimum*), the plant from which linen is made.

7

THE SECOND AIRT
OF THE
NORTHUMBRIAN RUNES

HAEGL-HAIL

The first rune of the second airt is Haegl, the ninth rune. The three runes at the beginning of this airt are icy and binding runes, expressing their place at the first part of winter in the year circle. Haegl represents the most powerful sacred number of the Northern Tradition, nine, "by the power of three times three." Literally, the rune's name means "hailstone." Hailstones are water transformed for a short while from its liquid into its solid phase, during which time it falls from the sky, sometimes so violently that it can destroy crops and property. But when the damage is done, the corns of hail melt, changing back into harmless, even beneficial, liquid water. *The Old English Rune Poem* puts it so: "Hail is the whitest of grains. It whirls from the heavens, scoured up by the wind, then transforms to water." As a general principle Haegl represents all aspects of frozen water that falls from the sky: sleet and snow as well as hail. Everyone who has experienced a bad winter will know the sudden transformation that a snowstorm can bring. Green fields and black roads are transformed rapidly into a sea of whiteness. Equally transformative is the reverse process of the thaw, when the colors of the landscape are restored and travel is eased.

Haegl is a rune of the unconscious mind and the formative processes of thought. On an impersonal level it is the rune at the roots of things, both on a physical, material level and in time. Thus it is used as a magical link between the upperworld and the Earth on which we walk, for Haegl is one of the major runes of "transvolution"; that is, the way things happen. It expresses those patterns of events in our past life that make the present what it is today. This rune can give us access to those patterns of energy originating in the past that are active in and affect the present time. It represents the power of evolution within the framework of present existence, whose direction can be altered by the magical action of Haegl. In divination Haegl thereby signifies those necessary processes that must occur for any project to succeed. Because of its icy nature Haegl can be used in *vardlokkur,* warding and binding magic, the area of expertise of the warlock. But Haegl is not the primary rune of magical binding; that is the main role of the next rune, Nyd. As a magical principle though, Haegl can instigate disruption, confusion, and chaos. Haegl is ruled by the deities who guard the passages linking the world of human consciousness with other planes. Haegl's corresponding tree is the yew (*Taxus baccata*), the oldest-lived European species, and its herb is bryony (*Bryonia alba*). Both have been used magically for access to the underworld and upperworld through the arts of shamanism and, more permanently, as a cause of death.

NYD—NEED

The tenth rune is called Nyd. The form of the rune represents the two balks of wood used for making the need-fire kindled at Beltane and in times of famine and pestilence. Nyd has the literal meaning of "need," both absence and scarcity of something and necessity. Primarily need is constraint, and magically it refers to binding, the "tight band across the chest" referred to in *The Old English Rune Poem.* But contained within the Nyd rune is the power to release one from need. Magically the use of Nyd calls for caution, and the wise adage "know thyself" is particularly applicable to this rune. When it is used magically the user must not attempt to strive against Wyrd but instead should use it in a constructive manner. So its main use in magic is for defensive binding spells, preventing magical attacks, and disempowering opponents. Nyd's trees are the rowan (*Sorbus aucuparia*) and the beech (*Fagus sylvatica*). The herb of the Nyd rune is snakeroot, or bistort (*Polygonum bistorta*).

IS–ICE

The eleventh rune is Is. Its shape is an icicle, vertical and fixed. It represents static existence, the present time, and, of course, all things frozen. Ice is the result of a change in state from liquid to solid. It comes from energy loss. "Ice is too cold, very slippery, its glassy glistening like a jewel, a floor formed of frost, fair to behold," says *The Old English Rune Poem.* Static resistance replaces fluidity. Is is the third rune that binds in the second airt. In magical usage Is is primarily a means of stopping activity. This rune is the polar opposite of the rune Cen. The quality expressed by Is does not only refer to motionlessness, for as well as being static, ice can move. When it does, as in a glacier, it does so with slow, irresistible force. Also, when it is in the form of an iceberg, the depth of floating ice is deceptive, for we can see only one-ninth of the true mass rising above the surface. When Is is used magically, although the results may initially seem small, the effects will contain unsuspected depths. So it is used to delay or halt the progress of something or to terminate a relationship. The corresponding tree of the Is rune is the alder (*Alnus glutinosa*), while its herb is the highly poisonous henbane

(*Hyoscyamus niger*), the *crann-gafainn* of the magical herbalism of the Scots-English borderlands.

GER–SEASON

Ger is the twelfth rune. It means "year" or "season," specifically referring to the cyclic nature of the seasons. Ger thereby signifies completion at the proper time. This rune can be used to bring forth a plentiful and rewarding harvest, but this can only happen after the right things have been done, according to the correct principles. Ger cannot act against the natural order of things, but if it is used in a proper way the results will be beneficial. And when appropriate it can speed up a process that is not proceeding quickly enough. The Northumbrian form of this rune is an upright stave, over which is written a circle or the diamond shape of the Ing rune. Figuratively this form represents the stable state once it has been achieved. It symbolizes the cosmic axis surrounded by the cycle of the year. In this form Ger is a pictographic representation of an actual object, the garland with its supporting pole, like traditional Maypoles. Ger's tree is the oak (*Quercus robur*), and its herb is rosemary (*Rosmarinus officinalis*).

EOH–YEW TREE

The thirteenth rune of the Northumbrian Futhork is Eoh, the yew tree rune. It represents a stave or sliver cut from a yew tree (*Taxus baccata*). This is one of the most magically powerful runes, the double-ended stave of life and death. The yew is the longest lived of all European trees. This is expressed in the power of Eoh as continuity and endurance. The yew is green throughout the year, never losing its needlelike leaves, but its bark, leaves, roots, fruit, and resin are all lethally poisonous. Because of this, numerologically, Eoh is "unlucky thirteen." But as it combines a remarkable longevity with toxicity, the yew is also seen as a tree of eternal life, for it possesses both the powers of death and regeneration.

On occasion older yew trees that have partially died are regenerated by their own daughter trees that grow in their decaying interiors. Also, certain yews have never-healing wounds. These are the bleeding yews, from which red resin flows like blood. Magically the yew and its rune have a number of related powers. Yew wood is a magical protector and facilitator in its own right. In former times the hook holding the cauldron above the cottage fire was fashioned of yew wood. The form of the rune is the shape of the household implement known as a hake, a hanger, or a pothook, which is used traditionally to suspend pots and kettles over the kitchen fire. This is alluded to in *The Old English Rune Poem,* which tells us, "On the outside, Yew is a rough tree, but strong and firm, the fire's guardian upheld by deep roots, a joy to the household." Made from iron by blacksmiths, these hooks are a development of the earlier wooden hooks. The hake is the embodiment of the rune Eoh, the dwelling of the house spirit, the master of the household. Blacksmiths use the same form to make wall anchors, whose often-reversed S-shape is sometimes fashioned into an iron snake or crossed to make a curving swastika. Wall anchors in this form, the double Eoh, magically prevent the house from being struck by lightning.

Fig. 7.1. Pothook in the form of Eoh

In addition to hakes, bows were also made of yew, so as a killer of animals and of humans, yew brought sudden death. In the times before firearms were invented, to carry a bow was a potent way of warding off any potential assailant. Because of this yew was physically as well as magically defensive. All the magical letter rows of the British Isles— Runic, Ogham, and the Aibitír of Gaelic—have this quality in the character that corresponds with the yew. In both the Anglo-Saxon and Northumbrian rune rows, yew as a bow has its own special stave, Yr. The Gaelic Aibitír too has two yew letters.

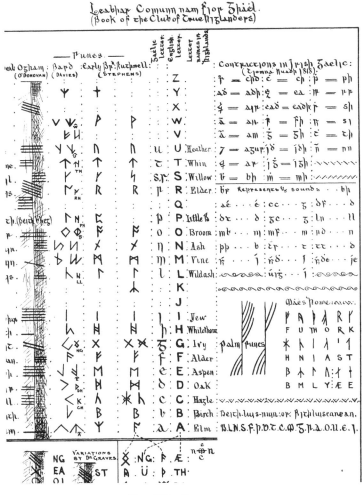

Fig. 7.2. Rune rows

In Northern Tradition magic another use for yew is in magic staves. Several ancient runic staves of yew survive from the runemasters of ancient Friesland. The runes on them employ the power of the yew wood to ward off and banish all harm, especially the powers of destruction and death. Yew staves, like the bow, can also be used for imposing one's will on other people, working both on the physical and on non-material planes. On a broader level yew protects the dead and provides the living with a means of access to the otherworld. Yew trees in churchyards and cemeteries, some of them older than the churches they accompany, are there to protect the dead. Druidic tradition speaks of the yew staff on which are written the powerful Ogham characters, which gives the practitioner the power to penetrate the kingdom of faërie without coming to any harm. Access to the otherworld through yew magic uses extremely risky life-or-death shamanic techniques, including ancient ecstatic-narcotic incense made from the resin or leaves of the yew. But the products of the yew tree are extremely toxic—potentially lethal—so the reader is strongly recommended not to make or use them. Using Eoh, we need not fear death, for through the yew we can gain passage from one state of being to another. The herb of Eoh is mandrake (*Mandragora officinarum*), a dread plant with a humanoid magic root.

ᛈ

PEORTH—A LIVELY TUNE

The fourteenth rune is Peorth, whose name is recalled in Celtic music to this day. In Irish traditional music the *poirt* is a sprightly tune, while its Scottish equivalent, the *port,* is described as a lively tune played on the bagpipes. The shape of the rune possibly represents a harp. But the most popular interpretation of Peorth is the dice cup, a medieval mechanism used for casting lots with dice. Yet another meaning given to this rune is a pawn or game piece. The lively tune, the dice, and the game piece represent the continually moving patterns of life. The port changes according to the chord progression of the tune while keeping the rhythmic pattern. Peorth as a playing piece in a board game represents the interaction between the freedom of our conscious willpower and the constraints of our surrounding conditions. When a tune or a game is played the rules of movement are already laid down, but beyond these limitations, the actual performance of the tune or game is dependent on the performer. The rules reflect the conscious skill and will of the individuals and their interactions during the music, song, dance, or game. Similarly in life too we are each in our own unique situation. But in the performance we have free will within the constraints of our own Wyrd: "Let us dree our Wyrd" is a Northumbrian expression for this.

Thus, through all its interpretations, Peorth is the power of Wyrd in the world, bringing forth its potential into physical manifestation. It is a rune of memory and recollection, problem solving and esoteric wisdom. Magically it gives access both to the inner secrets of the human world and to the inner workings of nature. It empowers us with the ability to distinguish things of value from those that are worthless. It is valuable in magical workings connected with initiation, where it can give meaningful insights into otherwise puzzling inner experiences. Peorth's corresponding trees are the beech (*Fagus sylvatica*) and the aspen (*Populus tremula*), while its herb is the lethal monkshood (*Aconitum napellus*).

ᛉ

EOLH-SECG—EELGRASS

A powerful rune of magical protection comes fifteenth in the rune row. It is the stave known as Eolh-Secg, whose shape symbolizes the stupendous resistant power of the elk. Magically this is the most powerful defensive "warding sign." It has the power of repelling all evil. *The Old English Rune Poem* tells us, "Eelgrass grows most often in the fen, waxes in the water, wounds grimly, with bleeding cuts burning one who tries to grasp it." Above all others it is the rune of personal protection.

Visualization of the rune around one's person provides a powerful protection against all kinds of physical and psychic attack. Equally it is effective in protecting property, especially buildings and vehicles. The magic warding power of Eolh-Secg promises protection against all of those forces or influences, known and unknown, that conflict with us. It is the power of the human striving toward divine qualities. Eolh-Secg's corresponding herb is the elongated sedge (*Carex elongata*), which is shaped like the rune and is very defensive against animals who would like to eat it. The Eolh-Secg rune's element is air. It corresponds with the magically powerful wood of the yew tree (*Taxus baccata*), along with the rare wild service tree (*Sorbus torminalis*). Like the yew, this tree also is protective but more specifically against wild things and people.

SIGEL–SUN

The last rune of the second airt is Sigel. This is a rune of great force that represents and channels the power of the sun. It signifies the triumph of light over darkness, bringing clarity and direction that helps us to achieve our objectives. As the power of sunlight and warmth, Sigel resists the forces of coldness, death, and disintegration. When it is used properly Sigel signifies the magical will acting for the benefit of all. Sigel can be used to direct power in a devastatingly straightforward manner. The rune's shape is like a lightning flash, and this describes its effects graphically. Because of this it is the rune for gaining victory by magical means. Its sacred trees are the juniper (*Juniperus communis*) and the bay (*Laurus nobilis*). Its magic herb is the semiparasitic plant mistletoe (*Viscum album*), one of the most sacred plants in the Celtic tradition, used to signify the rebirth of the sun from the darkness of midwinter at Yuletide.

8

THE THIRD AIRT
OF THE
NORTHUMBRIAN RUNES

↑

TIR–THE GUIDING STAR

Tir is the first rune of the third airt. Its spearlike shape symbolizes the targeting of positive forces in the correct place for the greatest effect. *The Old English Rune Poem* tells us that Tir "keeps faith well, is always on course over the darkness of night; it never fails." Tir is a god rune, for its name describes the power of the ancient Germanic sky god, known in England as Tîwaz and in Scandinavia as Tyr. In the Northern Tradition, Tir refers to the courageous Asa-Tyr, who gave his right hand to permit the gods to bind the destructive Fenris-Wolf, which had grown to such proportions that it threatened the cosmic order.

Tir is thus the rune of positive regulation, assisting one in the successful achievement of one's objectives. But when we use the Tir rune magically we must remember that achievement requires effort, which is self-sacrifice. Any success that comes from the use of Tir will inevitably be tempered by loss of some kind. A popular magical use of the Tir rune is in legal actions, but here success will come only if the litigant

Fig. 8.1. A doorknocker at All Saints' pavement church, York, depicting Fenris-Wolf swallowing Odin at Ragrnarök

is in the right to begin with. Travesties of justice, even when favorable to the magician, will not happen when Tir is used. Its tree is the oak (*Quercus robur*), and its magically effective herbs are Tir's helm (*Aconitum napellus*) and the purificatory sage (*Salvia officinalis*).

ᛒ
BEORC–BIRCH TREE

The eighteenth rune, representing the birch tree (*Betula pendula*), is Beorc. This rune's number is double the sacred nine of Haegl. In the Northern Tradition the number eighteen is symbolic of completion and new beginnings on a higher level. It marks the point at which the primal laws have been defined and manifested and at which the stage is set for the play of life to begin in earnest. As the first tree that recolonized the barren land when the ice retreated at the end of the last ice age, the birch thereby signifies regeneration. Magically Beorc is a rune of purification and new beginnings, empowering the female aspects of magic. It can be used to set the stage for a working, for the birch symbolizes cleansing and purification, apparent in the rebirth of the sun's vigor in springtime and on the physical level in the birch-twig brush of the besom. Using Beorc magically, we must have serious intentions. We should perform rune magic with Beorc only if we seriously intend to carry the working through to completion. Beorc helps us to create the movement that we need to undertake any task—more specifically, the task of life, which our Wyrd has set us. It is valuable at the beginning of a psychic journey. On a more basic level, we can use Beorc to assist any alteration in our lives, such as moving house. Beorc is identified with Beth, the first character of the Celtic tree alphabet. Its corresponding herb is lady's mantle (*Alchemilla xanthochlora*).

EH–HORSE

The nineteenth runestave is Eh, the horse rune. *The Old English Rune Poem* speaks of the horse as "the joy of peers, stepping out with pride when talked about by wealthy riders everywhere, and to the restless, always a comfort." The horse is a special animal, and consecrated horses were kept in the sacred enclosures of temples. Magically this horse rune is connected with combination, bringing things together into an unbreakable bond. But this requires absolute trust and loyalty between the horseman and the horse. Eh signifies more specifically the special skill of horsemanship, an ancient tradition whose late manifestation was in the Society of the Horseman's Word, which became specific in the use of horses in plowing from the eighteenth century onward in northern England and southern Scotland. This runestave has two sacred trees, the ash (*Fraxinus excelsior*) and the oak (*Quercus robur*). The Eh rune has the yellow-flowered ragwort (*Senecio jacobaea*) as its corresponding herb.

MAN–HUMAN BEING

Man is the twentieth runestave, signifying the basic qualities of humanness that we all possess, whether male or female. The Man rune is the shared experience of everybody's humanness. Its shape represents the archetypal human being in which all things are reflected: Man the Microcosm. As a rune of magical connection, Man is the symbolic embodiment of the social order, without which we cannot achieve our full human potential. Because language is the primary human quality, this is one of the *hogrunes,* the runes of the mind. Man is magically powerful in all areas of activity using language. It brings advantage in disputes and academic examinations.

The Old English Rune Poem tells us, "A man in his gladness is dear to his kin; yet each must fail the ones he loves, for the lord of judgment shall consign this unfortunate flesh to the Earth." Its related character in the alphabet of the Goths—Manna—means both "man" and "tree." This is from the Northern Tradition legend that the first humans were made from trees. Askr, the first man, came from an ash tree, and Embla, the first woman, an elm. The Man rune itself connects magically with the field maple tree (*Acer campestre*), the alder tree (*Alnus glutinosa*), and the holly tree (*Ilex aquifolium*). The herb of the Man rune is the madder (*Rubia tinctorum*), whose red pigment, *tiver,* is used to color runes.

LAGU–FLOWING WATER

The twenty-first rune represents water in its many phases and moods. This is Lagu, and the words *lagoon* and *lake* reflect some of the rune's aspects. But it is primarily a rune of fluidity. Lagu signifies the flowing power of the tides, the force of waterfalls, and the vigorous growth symbolized by the leek. Magically Lagu brings us into contact with the life force that is present in physical matter, organic growth, and waxing energies. Organic growth always proceeds in cycles, which can be seen in the growth rings of trees. This is manifested in Lagu as the ebb and flow of the tide, reminding us that, to be successful, we should use the rune only when the time is right. Lagu is used magically to clear blockages in progress and to accelerate any flow already taking place. Lagu's tree is the osier (*Salix viminalis*), and its herb is the leek (*Allium porrum*).

ING–ING

Ing is the twenty-second rune, a symbol of light, representing a fireplace, firebrand, or beacon. The *inglenook* in traditional Northumbrian farmhouses sheltering the fireplace is the place of Ing. The Ing rune is written with spreading lines that represent limitless expansion, carrying its energy outward into the surroundings, transmitting its light far and wide. Like Tir, Ing represents an eponymous god. He is the male consort of the Earth Mother of fertility and nurturing. *The Old English Rune Poem* tells us, "Ing was first seen by people among the East Danes; then afterward he went over the waves, following his wagon. Thus, the Heardings named this hero." Ing is the guardian of the hearth, so his rune is magically protective of households. Magically the Ing rune is a channel of potential energy, a doorway to the otherworld. Ing brings together and integrates the different elements in a magical working. We can use it also to obtain access to the power of limitless extension. Here, Ing requires a gradual buildup of energy for a period, before it is released as a single burst of power. Because of this, in sexual magic, it is connected with the force of the male orgasm. Ing's herb is self-heal (*Prunella vulgaris*), and its sacred tree is the apple (*Malus* spp.).

ETHEL–HOME

Ethel is the twenty-third rune of the Northumbrian Futhork. In the language of Frisia, from whence came the Anglo-Saxon runes, this rune is called Eeyen-eerde. This means "own earth" or "own land," which is a perfect definition of its meaning. Ethel has the form of an enclosure that is under the owner's control. *The Old English Rune Poem* says of this rune: "Home is loved by all people, if there rightfully and in peace we may enjoy many harvests in the hall." Beneficial energies can be drawn into this rune and kept there for later use. This is why Ethel is used as a sigil carved beneath the gable end of houses. Ethel's magic is most effective in the areas of personal belongings and ancestral heritage. It brings magical workings into manifestation on the earthly level, being the center through which the magic can operate. As an operating principle the Ethel rune strengthens our connections with other people in our group or family. Thus Ethel is powerful in maintaining the existing state of things. It resists arbitrary rules and preserves individual and clan liberty within the framework of natural law. Its tree is the hawthorn (*Crataegus monogyna*), used for hedging enclosures, and its herb is the white clover (*Trifolium repens*), especially in its lucky four-leafed form.

DAEG–DAY

Daeg is the twenty-fourth rune, meaning "day." Its form represents the dynamic balance between polarities, especially light and darkness. Daeg is magically a powerful blocking rune, but it is not harmful. On the contrary, it is a very beneficial rune of light, health, prosperity, and openings. Daeg is described in *The Old English Rune Poem* as "day, the Lord's message, dear to men." Some Old English sundials using the octaval tide

Fig. 8.2. Daeg wall anchor   Fig. 8.3. Daeg posts

system of time-measurement mark the beginning of the working day, 7:30 a.m., by a Daeg rune. Shutters and doors in the Netherlands and Frisia traditionally are painted with the Daeg glyph. Rune lore teaches that the Daeg glyph signifies a stable balance between the opposite states of light and darkness, opening and closing. As the door, Daeg allows entry of favorable things and keeps out the unwelcome.

As well as on doors and shutters, the Daeg glyph is the traditional stamp on blacksmiths' ironwork, particularly strapwork on doors. It is also painted or carved on doorposts and other uprights in a house, most notably in the traditional farmhouses of Ryedale and Eskdale in Yorkshire. From 1936 onward posts carved with this glyph have been called witch posts. Before then they were known as speer posts or heck posts from their location supporting the timber screen, with seats next to the inglenook fireplace. The glyph carved very visibly on the post was made to protect the house and hearth against the evil eye, curses, and destructive magic in general. Daeg thus prevents the entry of harmful sprites into the house or room, while admitting powers and people who are desirable. Another magical use is to conceal; things and people marked with this rune are not actually invisible, but they are not noticed. On a more transcendent level, Daeg gives us access to cosmic consciousness. Its trees are the oak (*Quercus robur*) and the Norway spruce (*Picea abies*). Its herb is clary sage (*Salvia horminoides*).

9

THE FOURTH AIRT
OF THE
NORTHUMBRIAN RUNES

ᚪ

AC—OAK TREE

The fourth Northumbrian airt commences with the twenty-fifth rune, Ac, which represents the oak, the holy tree of the god of sky and thunder, in the British tradition, Daronwy, Thunor, and Thor. Ac is a rune of great potential power and many uses. *The Old English Rune Poem* expresses them: "On this Earth, Oak is useful to men. It is fodder for pigs, and often it sails on the Gannet's bath, where the spear-sharp sea tests the worthiness of the timber." The potential power of Ac is symbolized by the acorn, from which the mighty oak tree emanates. Although seemingly insignificant, this small seed contains within itself the awesome potential of massive growth and longevity. Magically Ac is the cosmic egg, which channels the power of strong, continuous growth, from small beginnings to a mighty climax. We use Ac to reinforce magic that assists the creative and productive processes. Ac's corresponding herb is hemp (*Cannabis sativa*).

ᚫ
AESC—ASH TREE

Aesc, the "god rune," is the fourth stave in the Elder Futhark but placed twenty-sixth in the Northumbrian. Aesc is the ash tree (*Fraxinus excelsior*), one of the most sacred trees of the Northern Tradition. The black buds and horseshoe-shaped leaf scars of the ash denote its dedication to Woden. The universal world tree, Yggdrasil, the cosmic axis linking the worlds, is an ash. It is a symbol of stability. *The Old English Rune Poem* tells us, "Humans love the Ash tree, towering high. Though many enemies come forth to fight it, it keeps its place steadfastly, in a firm position." Aesc originated long before the runes, in ancient Indo-European culture. In the Vedic tradition it is the Sanskrit primal sound, which created the present universe. This is the divine breath, called in the Northern Tradition *önd*. This power actually exists and is the divine source present within the human being. Aesc is thus a powerful controller of the consciousness and all intellectual activities. Magically this rune also invokes the divine force and is used in workings that aim to maintain and reinforce the natural order. As well as the ash, this rune also is connected magically with the linden tree (*Tilia platyphyllos*). The Aesc rune's herb is the fly agaric mushroom (*Amanita muscaria*).

YR—YEW BOW

Yr is the twenty-seventh rune of Northumbria. It represents a yew bow, both a weapon and an instrument of divination. When the rune Yr is used it takes over this aspect of the yew tree from Eoh in the twenty-four rune row of the Elder Futhark. The form of the rune has been seen as representing the arbalest, or crossbow, a more powerful form of bow used in ancient times for hunting and military combat. The oldest known representation of a crossbow is on a Pictish stone in Scotland. The Yr rune as a human-made weapon more generally represents handicraft. Craft is the perfect combination of skills and knowledge applied to materials provided by nature, and, of course, the practice of archery is a highly skilled craft. As well as being a death-bringer, the bow was used for divination. There were two different ways of using the bow to find a special place. One was to shoot an arrow, the place sought being marked by where the arrow fell. This technique appears in the legend of Robin Hood, for the locations of his grave and that of Little John were defined by arrow shot. Magically Yr is used both defensively, as protection at the expense of others, and for finding the correct location for anything, being literally on target. Yr magic is most valuable in finding lost objects or the best place for anything. The herbs of this rune are the black-berried bryony (*Bryonia alba*) and mandrake (*Mandragora officinarum*).

IOR—WATER BEAST

Ior is the twenty-eighth rune, signifying a water beast. Ior denotes the dual nature of matter, symbolized by the amphibious habits of many water beasts. More specifically, Ior signifies the sea serpent, a beast once well-known to mariners but now endangered or extinct. In the Northern Tradition, Ior is personified as the World Serpent, whose name is Iormungand. According to the Northern Tradition, Iormungand is extremely formidable and dangerous. Thor fishes for Iormungand using an ox head as bait. He succeeds in hooking it, but before he can drag it from the water the giant with whom Thor is fishing cuts the rope, and Iormungand sinks back to the ocean floor. Symbolically this means that if it ever became possible to eliminate the dangerous qualities that Iormungand represents, then inevitably this would produce a catastrophe far worse than the consequences of its continued existence. Ior thus symbolizes those unavoidable hardships and problems with which we must come to terms so that our lives can be tolerable. Like Ior, these supernatural beasts represent certain forces in nature that, rather than being killed, are quelled. Then, still living, they are integrated with the human-natural order. This tale of Thor is a fine example of the law of the unity of opposites in the Northern Tradition and their integration into their appropriate places in life. Unfortunately the modern response to such dangerous forces as these is to seek to eliminate them completely, which is impossible. The Northumbrian worm legends are instances of the power of Ior. Magically Ior is a binding rune of great power, as is one of the rune's corresponding trees, the ivy (*Hedera helix*). The ivy is obviously a plant of binding and tying. While it is said to strangle and kill other trees, it remains evergreen, making it a plant of life and death. Ior represents the serpentine, binding power of the water snake, the seaweed kelp (*Laminaria digitata*), by which swimmers are sometimes entangled and drowned. The corresponding tree of Ior is the linden (*Tilia platyphyllos*), connected in Germanic tradition with the Lindwurm serpent.

EAR—DUST

Ear is the twenty-ninth rune of the Northumbrian Futhork and the final one of the Anglo-Saxon Futhark. Ear is the soil of the earth, the dust to which our bodies return at death. Ear is thus symbolic of the grave, the termination of human life. But without an end there could never have been a beginning: without death there cannot be life. Ear thereby signifies the unavoidable end of all things, more specifically the inevitable return of individual, living human beings to the earth of which our bodies are made. As *The Old English Rune Poem* tells us, "The dust is frightening to every nobleman, when the flesh suddenly starts to cool, and the body must choose the Earth as a bleak bedfellow. Bright fruits fall, joys cease, relationships pass away." Magically Ear brings things to a close, more specifically accelerating the arrival of an inevitable end point, a useful rune for bringing about the swift conclusion of something that the user requires to be terminated. Ear is the third yew-tree rune, along with Eoh and Yr. Its herb is equally deadly, being the lethal hemlock (*Conium maculatum*).

CWEORTH–RITUAL FIRE

The thirtieth rune is Cweorth. This character, which appears only in the Northumbrian rune row, is related to the Ogham character Quert, the Apple Tree of the Celtic tree alphabet. Like Quert, Cweorth has the meaning of rebirth and eternal life. Specifically, this rune signifies the swirling, ascending flames of a ritual fire. Cweorth denotes ritual cleansing by means of fire, the process of transformation by burning. In the case of the funeral pyre, one of Cweorth's aspects, fire serves to liberate the spirit from the material body so that it can be reborn in a new form. More commonly Cweorth represents the festival bonfire of celebration, joy, and liberation. Thus Cweorth is the opposite of the binding need fire of Nyd. Magically this thirtieth rune can be used to bring about all kinds of transformation. The corresponding trees of Cweorth are the bay (*Laurus nobilis*), the beech (*Fagus syhatica*), and, through its Celtic connection, the apple (*Malus* spp.). The sacred herb of Cweorth is rue, or herb of grace (*Ruta graveolens*), used in rites of purification.

CALC–CUP

The thirty-first rune of the Northumbrian Futhork, the penultimate character of the fourth airt, is Calc. This rune has the literal meaning of "a ritual container" or "an offering cup," such as the maple-wood wassail bowl used in the rites of Yuletide and the spiritual vessels in Celtic and Christian mythology, such as the Cauldron of Wisdom and the Holy Grail. The cup or chalice is the object of the quest, as in Arthurian legend. So the rune's meaning is concerned with the natural, successful, conclusion of a process. Magically Calc signifies the successful conclusion of a working, so it is appropriate to use it in a closing rite. Once it is over, the transformation has been achieved, and no more needs to be done. Calc can also be used magically in contacting absent friends or the departed in an act of remembrance, as we do when we drink to absent friends or in honor of the spirits of the dead. The magical trees of the Calc rune are the field maple (*Acer campestre*), the tree from which sacred cups are turned. The other sacred tree of Calc is the quicken tree, or rowan (*Sorbus aucuparia*). Calc's sacred herb is milfoil, or yarrow (*Achillea millefolium*).

STAN–STONE

Stan is the final rune of the fourth airt. It has the meaning of "stone," containing the magical power of stone in all its forms. At a basic level Stan represents the bones of the Earth, the ground beneath our feet. It can signify a blockage, such as a rock lying across a path or a stone at

Fig. 9.1. Northumbrian wyrdstone

the entrance to a cave. Additionally Stan represents a megalith standing at a place of power in the landscape, a wyrdstone bearing natural runes, which we can read, or a stone or playing piece in a board game.

Stan's shape is that of the stone or bone playing pieces used in ancient Northern Tradition board games such as *hnefatafl*. Magically Stan can be used to forge a spiritual link between human beings and between earthly and heavenly powers. In its appearance as a game piece or a geomantic stone Stan can either provide protection or act as a block to our progress. An important magical use is in blocking and stopping, turning back opposition, and driving away assailants. *The Lay of Hamdir* tells of a Stan spell by the High Gods' Kinsman (Woden/Odin).

> *Roared he as bears roar;*
> *"Stones to the stout ones,*
> *That the spears bite not,*
> *Nor the edges of steel,*
> *These sons of Jonakr!"*

Stan is here the rune of magical turning and blocking, which can also be turned for use in attack and punishment. And of course the stone is the oldest offensive missile known to humans. The corresponding trees of Stan are the blackthorn (*Prunus spinosa*) and the witch hazel (*Hamamelis mollis*). Stan's magical herb is the stone-loving lichen known as Iceland moss (*Cetraria islandica*).

GAR–SPEAR

The thirty-third and final rune of Northumbria is Gar, which has the literal meaning of "spear." More specifically, Gar refers to the spear carried by Woden. The Northern Tradition teaches that Woden's spear has a staff of ash wood, symbolically linking it with the world tree,

Yggdrasil. Unlike the other thirty-two runes, which are assigned to their corresponding airt, Gar stands outside. This is because it is the central point, the stable axis, which is simultaneously internal, external, everywhere, and nowhere. When the runes of the four airts are written out, Gar is written at the center, and all the other runes are laid out in a circle around it. But holding the center is not the only function of Gar. It can also be used to magically empower the beginning of a new order of things and as a rune of fulfillment. In this way it serves as the seal in the completion of a magical formula or working. As a sigil it represents the final affirmation of the working. Its most useful function magically, however, is in wiping out any runic onlays that are no longer needed. Gar's corresponding trees are the ash (*Fraxinus excelsior*) and the now-rare spindle tree (*Euonymus europaea*), once used, as its name suggests, for making spindles used in the preparation of thread for weaving and sewing, thus linking us again to the Web of Wyrd.

10
RUNES IN MAGIC AND ENCRYPTION

RUNES AND MAGIC

Rune magic works on a system of correspondences, for each stave encapsulates a true principle that is discernable within the Web of Wyrd. For example there are certain elements that rule each rune. These come from the five-element system of the Northern Tradition: fire, air, water, earth, and ice. Each rune has a polarity, either masculine or feminine. There are also divinities who are the major rulers of each rune. Each rune has a corresponding herb and tree that are linked symbolically and magically with the most important quality of the rune. We can use the corresponding wood or herb to empower the rune working.

In addition to this direct use, Northern Tradition scripture tells us of the wonderful scope of rune magic. The words of Odin, recorded and systematized in *Hávamál*, speak of eighteen different power spells. Earlier Anglo-Saxon writings show that many of these spells were being used in England centuries before they were written down as this text in Iceland:

> *Nine power spells I learned from the noted son*
> *Of Bestla's father, Bolthorn: And a drink I took*
> *Of the precious mead poured out of Othrerir.*

Then I became fruitful; to grow and thrive.
Word sought word after word in me:
Spell sought spell after spell in me.

Runes you will find, and skillful characters;
Wry great characters, very strong characters;
That a mighty thule painted, and great gods made,
Carved by the prophet of the gods.

Odin among gods but Dain for elves
And Dvalin for dwarves,
Asviðr for giants:
Some I carved myself.

Do you know how to carve them?
Do you know how to read them?
Do you know how to paint them?
Do you know how to prove them?
Do you know how to pray with them?
Do you know how to sacrifice with them?
Do you know how to send with them?
Do you know how to offer with them?

It is better not to pray at all than to sacrifice too much:
A gift always demands a repayment.
It is better not to send at all than to offer too much:
Thus Thund* carved before the birth of nations
At that point he began when he came back.

I know those spells which no lord's wife knows,
Nor any man's son.

---

*Thund is a by-name of Odin.

One is called Help, and it will help you
Against sorrows and ordeals and every grief there is.

I know the second, which those sons of men need
Who wish to live as healers.

I know the third:
If my need grows dire
For binding my deadly enemies, I dull the blades
Of my foes—neither weapon nor deception will bite for
    them.

I know this, the fourth:
If warriors tie up
My arms, I call this,
And I can go free: the shackles break from my feet,
And the handcuffs from my hands.

I know this, the fifth:
If I see an arrow shot in combat,
Shot deadly straight,
None flies so hard that I cannot stop it
If I catch sight of it.

I know this, the sixth:
If a lord curses me by the roots of a fresh young tree,
The man who calls down curses on me
Misfortunes will destroy him, rather than me.

I know this, the seventh:
If I see a high hail on fire around my comrades,
None burns so fiercely that I cannot rescue them;
I know the spell to chant.

I know this, the eighth:
Which is useful for everyone to learn,
Whose hatred grows for a war-king's sons:
I can soon change that.

I know this, the ninth:
If I need to keep my ship floating,
I can calm the wind, smooth the waves,
And lull the sea to sleep.

I know this, the tenth:
If I see the hedge riders magically flying high,
I can make it so that they go astray
Of their own skins, and of their own souls.

I know this, the eleventh:
If I must lead old friends to battle,
I call under their shields, and they go empowered,
Safe to war, safe from war, safe wherever they are.

I know this, the twelfth:
If I see a body swinging from a noose high in a tree,
Then I carve and I color the runes,
So that the man comes down and speaks with me.

I know this the thirteenth,
If I should sprinkle water on a young lord,
He will not fall, no matter if he goes to war:
The hero will not go down beneath the swords.

I know this, the fourteenth:
If I should preach of the gods at a moot,
I will know how to distinguish between all gods and elves:

Few of the unwise know this.

I know this, the fifteenth,
Which the dwarf Thjothrerir
Called before Delling's doors.
He chanted power to the gods and strength to elves,
And foresight to Hroptatyr.

I know this, the sixteenth:
If I want to have the wise woman's spirited games,
I steal the heart of a white-armed wench
And I turn all her thoughts.

I know this, the seventeenth:
So that the young woman will not want to avoid me.

Loddfafnir you will be long in learning these lays,
Though they will do you good if you get them,
Be usable if you can grasp them,
Handy if you have them.

I know this, the eighteenth,
Which never will I teach maid or man's wife
(It is better to understand it alone: the end of the poem
*   follows),*
Except that woman who embraces me in her arms,
Or perhaps my sister.

Now are the Hávamál sung in Hávi's Hall,
Essential to the sons of men, useless to the sons of giants.
Hale he sang, hale he who understands.
May he use them well who has grasped them,
Hale those who have listened."

This list of rune spells covers every possibility: there are binding spells, love spells, battle magic, binding magic, protection against harm, and the means to distinguish beneficial divinities from harmful sprites. They are the basis for all rune magic. The fourth charm, allowing prisoners of war to free themselves, is recorded in a story from Bede. In seventh-century England this technique was used, and runes were its empowerment. The event took place after the Battle of the Trent, fought between the Northumbrians and the Mercians in the year 679. Northumbrian forces had been worsted, and the survivors had been compelled to withdraw. Imma, a young Northumbrian nobleman, had been felled in the slaughter and lay unconscious in a heap of corpses. But after the battle had ended he regained consciousness and got to his feet, and then he wandered about trying to find the Northumbrian army again. But he was discovered by Mercian soldiers, who took him to their leader. Imma understood that if the Mercians discovered that he was a member of the Northumbrian nobility, he would be killed in revenge, for a blood feud had triggered the battle. So Imma told the Mercians that he was a churl who had been conscripted into carrying supplies for the military. The Mercians believed him and tended his wounds, waiting for him to build up his strength again until they could decide on his fate, perhaps selling him as a slave. After a while he regained some strength, so they shackled him at night to prevent him running away. As soon as his guards left him his fetters fell off. The Mercian leader, being told of the event, asked Imma if he had got any loosening letters that he was keeping hidden. By this Bede meant loosening runes, carved on staves concealed about his body.

11

MAGICAL SYMBOLS AND ARTIFACTS OF OLD NORTHUMBRIA

HAEGL: NINE, THE MAGIC NUMBER OF THE NORTH

The cosmology of the Northern Tradition tells of the Nine Worlds. Odin hung on the windswept tree for nine days and nine nights before receiving the runes. A common spell to empower a magical working is "By the power of three times three." That magical animal, the cat, is said to have nine lives, and the waves of incoming tide come in groups of nine. In Northumbria the board game Nine Men's Morris has survived as a village game played continuously since ancient times. The Lambton Worm had nine spiracles on either side of its head; it made nine circuits when it spiraled around its hill and needed the milk from nine cows every day. The curse of the Worm fell on the Lambton family for nine generations. Likewise the otherwise invulnerable Lourd Soulis was boiled to death in a cauldron on Nine Stane Rigg inside a stone circle composed of nine stones. Another magic hill in the area of Old Northumbria is Nine Standards Rigg. In the mid-nineteenth century, when the shipbuilders of Sunderland went on strike and won their

Fig. 11.1. The Lambton Worm's nine spiracles

cause in one day, it was celebrated in Joe Wilson's song "The Lads Upon the Wear!" as the Nine Hours' Strike.

In contemporary rune magic the Northern Tradition cord has nine knots. Each one stands for one of the nine worlds of the runic cosmos. It is made of red cord one ell in length, protected with a shielding spell, and nine knots are tied in it at equal distances along the cord. The knots are tied with this incantation: "By knot of one, it is begun, by knot of two, the power comes through, by knot of three, so must it be, by knot of four, the power will store, by knot of five, the power's alive, by knot of six, the power to fix, by knot of seven, the power to leaven, by knot of eight, ties up the fate, by knot of nine, what's done is mine."

RINGS OF POWER

All rings, no matter how large or how small, are circles of power. A ring is symbolic of eternity, wholeness, the circle that has no beginning and no end. Rings from the natural world are recognized as objects of power. The holed stones called hagstones or holeystones have been used as magical protectors since ancient times. It is the custom to hang one in stable, byre, and house by a string of flax. Especially powerful are hagstone chains—rings of rings. Holed standing stones and holes through stones in buildings are traditionally held in reverence as places of healing and foresight. Stone circles are another form of magic ring, used long after their original building for various purposes that need magical protection, such as folk-moots, trials, and executions. In 1820, William Danby built a stone circle on the moors at Masham in Yorkshire, close to Ripon. The Ilton Circle is a complex structure of many stones and Stonehenge-like trilithons, built for unknown purposes, but in an age when secret societies abounded. Like the ancient stone rings, the Ilton Circle is a place where human consciousness is subtly altered.

In former times it was traditional to gather together bystanders to witness a legal act, such as swearing an oath or paying a debt. They would form a ring, at the middle of which the act was done. It is a secular version of the magic circle cast by all magicians to enclose the power of their workings and to exclude unwanted influences. Dancing around the Maypole in a ring is a contemporary continuation of the tradition. On a planetary scale, the Arctic Circle, known in Old Norse as Hjol-Gadds-Ringr, was seen as a sacred enclosure inside which the awesome phenomenon of the midnight sun can be witnessed. The actual name of this circle is a word of power in rune magic.

Every smith-forged metal ring is emblematic of the wholeness of eternity, like the alchemical serpent biting its own tail. The ancient Germanic epic poem the *Nibelungenlied* is centered on a sacred ring of power. Finger rings are most associated with rune magic, and several have come down to us from old Northumbria. The key element in

J. R. R. Tolkien's books *The Hobbit* and *The Lord of the Rings* is the ring. Tolkien took his model for his fictional rings from the real ancient runic magic rings that actually exist. Surviving rings of the first millennium are of several types, not only metallic. It is possible that there were wooden rings, but these would have been less durable than precious metal. Three runic rings in the British Museum have obvious magical inscriptions. One, found in 1817 on Greymoor Hill, Kingmoor, near Carlisle, is made of gold. It is beautifully engraved with Northumbrian runes that read ÆRÜRIUFLTÜRIURIThONgLÆSTÆPON inscribed on the outside and TOL on the inside. Another ring of unknown origin, but with a known history since 1745, also in the British Museum, has an identical inscription. This ring is made of bronze. The third example is a ring carved from agate. It too has a magical inscription: ERÜRIUFDOL ÜRIURIThOL WLESTEPOTENOL. These are finger rings of power, intended to be worn for magical purposes.

Fig. 11.2. Magic rune ring of gold, Cumbria

Fig. 11.3. Magic rune ring of agate

RUNIC CODES IN NORTHUMBRIA

The fragment of a Northumbrian stone cross kept in the church at Hackness, near Scarborough, Yorkshire, has runic inscriptions in a number of cryptic systems. Many ancient runic inscriptions are in code, for the runes have the most complex cryptic lore of any alphabet. Putting a magical formula in code is very practical. It prevents others from reading the meaning and also stops other rune users from attempting to alter the course of the magic. The most basic runic code writes the runes from right to left. Today this is called "mirror writing." Runes written in the wrong direction are called wend runes. In ancient days when few were literate but many more were semiliterate and could make out letters, writing runes the other way may have been enough to baffle many people. The most skilled runemasters went further than just writing backward; they used various means of encryption. A popular method substituted one letter for another, the simplest form of which moved the whole alphabet one letter in either direction. Thus the name Nigel will be written with the runes *Hnibm* if the preceding letter is substituted, or *Igzmng* if the following letter replaces each one. Either way, an apparently meaningless jumble of letters is created. This method was often used to encode individual names. Another type of encryption substitutes one character for another. This can be done either letter by letter or systematically by corresponding groups of runes. There are many ways of doing this. One ancient method is known from the runic code stick excavated in the Bryggen, the docklands of Bergen in Norway. This stick is the key to a code that uses multiple letters to represent individual ones. Code sticks were made by runemasters to enable them to write messages that only they, or others with the key tothe code, could read. Similar code sticks were used by the Celtic Druids. Scottish plaid weavers record their patterns on sett sticks, which encode the patterns for the clans' tartans in the simplest way, using the correct number of threads of the right color in the proper sequence.

Branch runes are another encryptive technique that uses number symbols that indicate the position of a letter in a prearranged group. There are several ways of doing this. It can be done simply by indicating the number of the letter from the beginning of the alphabet, as for example in the Roman alphabet the number *3* represents *C*. But unlike the Roman alphabet, the Elder Futhark is divided into three airts and the Northumbrian Futhork four, and the number symbols are based on this. The rune row is divided into its three or four airts, which are numbered *1, 2, 3, 4*. Inside each airt each rune is given a number, counted forward, backward, or according to some other sequence. Two numbers thus denote each letter. It is usual to place the airt's number first and then the rune's number. The most common way of writing branch runes is as an upright stave with side branches pointing upward. On one side the number of branches represents the number of the airt from which the rune comes. On the other side the number of branches represents the number of the rune in that airt. For example, a branch rune that bears three strokes to the left and two to the right represents the second rune of the third airt. Thus, for example, the name Nigel would be denoted by the numbers *2,2; 2,3; 2,4; 3,3; 3,5.* Cryptic runes of this kind can be seen on the cross fragment at Hackness, near Scarborough.

These rune codes are related closely to the Celtic Ogham characters. This type of code includes the branch runes (*kvistrünar*), the tree runes (*hahalruna*), and the tent runes (*tjaldrünar*). The side branches on tree runes point upward, while those of tree runes point downward. But whichever way they are written, the principle is the same, representing the airt number on one side and the rune number on the other. Tent runes are based on X-shaped forms. They are usually read clockwise, beginning at the left, using the same principle as the others. Another type of encryption is the Iis runes. They also use numbers to denote individual runes. But unlike the branch, tree, and tent runes, the Iis runes are arrays of single strokes that are not connected to one another. To represent the number of the airt, the Iis runes use short strokes. Longer strokes denote the number of each rune within the airt.

By these and more complex methods, the ancient northern skalds and runemasters were able to hide messages for those who could decode them. Runes and Ogham characters appear together in *The Book of Ballymote,* written in Ireland in 1391.

KNOTS, KNOTWORK, AND MEANINGFUL PATTERNS

We usually visualize the Web of Wyrd as a woven fabric made on a loom. But equally it can be visualized as a series of threads knitted together, for it is a metaphor and not a physical object. Knots are the means to tie things up magically as well as physically, and they are the means by which garments are knitted. The creation of the net was an early human craft triumph derived from the invention of the knot. Seen as a catchall, trapping fish in the sea, beasts on land, and birds of the air, the net became an extension of the human hand. A Northern Tradition story tells how the trickster Loki was caught and bound after he invented the net and then burned it lest his enemies should discover the new secret tool. But those who hunted him saw the pattern of the net in the ashes and, making one, ensnared its inventor. Woven nets that entangle and ensnare act as artificial enclosures, as with the traditional ways of penning in animals, fencing villages, and making the walls of buildings by weaving wattle hurdles. They are not flexible spun threads, but grass, straw, and branches of trees, split to the right flexibility, can form upright zales between which are woven horizontal rods. Just as the woven fabric clothes the body, the woven wattle protects humans from the weather and domesticated animals from predators.

Knots made in rope, cord, and netting for practical and magical purposes, as well as women's hair braiding, and interlaces made during performances such as sword dancing, are transitory, and there are few surviving examples from ancient times. Some of the knotwork carved on stone and wood, tooled onto leather, and drawn in manuscripts has survived. Today this artistic knotwork is called Celtic art, after the books of J. Romilly Allan, John G. Merne, and George Bain popularized it to an audience in the first half of the twentieth century. But much of this in Northumbria, as in the Isle of Man, was in an English or Norse context, and many patterns are common to Ireland, Wales, Scotland, and England.

Binding spells are intended to be the equivalent of physical knots, making nets and ropes that tie up the designated target. European folklore records that interlacing patterns, also called knots, serve to bind bad luck and ward off the causes of bad luck. They enclose and bind the harmful influences, disempowering them. Northern Tradition myth tells how powerful destructive beings are captured and bound by the godly powers of proper order. *Gylfaginning,* the first part of *The Edda,* tells of the binding of both the Fenris-Wolf and Loki by magical means. Christian eschatology too describes the binding of the devil in chains for a thousand years. A carving of the bound devil exists in Stonegate, York.

Fig. 11.4. Traditional sword dancing at Kirkby Malzeard Lock

The tradition of making cat's cradles from string is usually thought of as a children's game. Yet identical patterns are part of the repertoire of binding magic. In Scandinavia they are called *troll-knutar,* part of a northern circumpolar tradition of string magic linked to shamanic practices. The northern English and Scots word *warlock,* meaning "a cunning man or practitioner of spellcraft," is rarely used today except pejoratively. Because dictionary definitions have given it meanings such as "liar" and "deceiver," it has fallen from use, but it is clear that in reality it relates to the power to shut in or enclose; that is, a person with the capability of making binding spells. The power of the warlock is to make knots, physical or psychic, to ward off evil spirits and to lock up or bind their effects.

Knots also exist as sigils and signs. With a central cross loop the fourfold loop appears on English clog almanacs as the sigil of All Saints' Day, November 1, so it has become the sigil for Samhain in the present-day Paganism. The names given to knots are, as one would expect, confused. In 1947 a variant of this knot was described on a wooden vessel found at Setesdal in Norway and called *valknute.* But the name *valknute, valknut,* or *valknútr* is more commonly used for the three interlaced equilateral triangles that were carved on some memorial stones on Gotland and on rings and other Viking-age metalwork from England. It is associated with the god Odin as "the knot of the slain."

The skills of self-making are essential in traditional society. The rural poor, and those whose work was free, individual, or in some way not allied to the urban collective, such as carters, drovers, keel and sloop men, and fishermen and fishwives, retained personal craft skills that were downgraded in towns by the industrial revolution. Their home-knitted garments and self-made tools and utensils were often considered "rustic" or "rural" by urban dwellers and inferior to manufactured goods. But embedded in the country and coastal crafts were traditions that stretched back to the runic era and beyond, the meaningful symbolism and magic of making and the made affirming the positive values of continuity and self-reliance.

Knitwear is strongly associated with this part of Britain, as hardy sheep have been herded here for thousands of years. The patterns on traditional knitwear have customary meanings, a vast repertoire of patterns that vary from place to place. Unfortunately the prevalence of machine-made ganseys and jerseys in the twenty-first century means that many of the traditional knitted patterns used by the fishermen of Old Northumbria in earlier days are no longer preserved. And the decline of the fishing industry too has broken up the communities that sustained the tradition in former times. Those that do exist are continuing emblems of local identity. Various patterns from Patrington, Flamborough, Scarborough, Whitby, Staithes, Cullercoats, Newbiggin, Amble, and Seahouses are preserved, and new ganseys are knitted according to these traditions. Runic elements are present in some of them. Also extant are the jersey patterns of the keel and sloop men on the inland waterways around the River Humber as far south as Lincoln and Nottingham to Leeds and Huddersfield in the west and Boroughbridge, Yeldingham, and Driffield in the north. They include moss stitch and chevron patterns, the tree of life, hexagrams, diamonds, and checkered patterns.

12
ING

Legendary and Magical History

THE MAGICAL ELEMENTS IN THESE ACCOUNTS are discounted by academic historians because they do not fit in with their narratives. Equally, with accounts of holy people and saints, the miraculous parts of their stories are unacceptable, even to many clerics. So they have been expunged from history. But all history in the days before the rise of the academic historian was infused with supernatural and magical events—*ostenta*—the workings of gods and providence. Magical and supernatural events were accorded equal status with events that appear mundane. The legendary history of every nation is full of such accounts, and scriptures held as sacred by their devotees are almost entirely composed of such legendary history. The stories of the Celtic saints, for example, run the whole gamut of supernatural happenings: divination, ostenta, oracles, distant viewing, apparitions of angels and otherworldly beasts, the use of magical objects, healings, bilocation, teleportation, psychic battles with demons, and divine intervention. These stories encapsulate the practices of magic and the mantic arts of the period, which were then integral parts of everyday life, for the magical worldview was present among all, regardless of the ethnicity or religion to which they belonged.

Of course Northumbrian history and legend contain a number of such events in the lives of royalty and aristocracy as well as the Celtic and English holy men who lived there. *Flores historiarum* (Flowers of History), written around the reign of King Edward I, purportedly by the Benedictine monk Matthew of Westminster, recounts the story of King Edwin. In Edwin's time, the early seventh century, Britain was a battleground fought over by many conflicting religious and ethnic factions. There were three different religions led by three significant kings. Cadwallon, who had the title of king of Britain, was ethically British, what now would be called Welsh. He was a Celtic Christian. King Edwin, an ethnic Anglian, king of Northumbria, was a convert from Germanic paganism to Catholic Christianity. Catholic Christianity in those days was part of the Orthodox Church, but as Northumbria is in Western Europe, that part of the church was subject to Rome. Rome split away from the Orthodox Church in the year 1054 when there was an argument as to which patriarch should be the supreme ruler of the religion. In the seventh century England's official religion was Orthodox, a branch of the Christian religion now only associated with Eastern Europe and Africa with the Greek, Russian, Serbian, Armenian, and Ethiopian Orthodox churches. King Penda, also ethnically Anglian and the king of the land to the south of Northumbria, Mercia, was a staunch follower of his ancestral religion, the Germanic pagan gods and ways.

In the year 633 the army of Cadwallon, king of the Britons, fought Edwin's forces and suffered a heavy defeat. Cadwallon and his remnant forces fled to Ireland, from whence they attempted several returns to northern Britain. But every time they attempted to land, Edwin's forces were ready and waiting. This ability to know where Cadwallon's forces were was put down to astrology. For among King Edwin's entourage was an astrologer called Pellitus, who came from the area of modern Spain. Edwin appears to have conducted his wars with the aid of Pellitus, who told him the most auspicious times and perhaps places to fight battles. Earlier King Edwin had founded his capital at Yeavering, then called Gefrin, the Hill of Goats, where modern excavators found a burial of a man with a staff and a goat's skull, believed to be a foundation sacrifice. It is not known what or where the foundation sacrifice of Edwinsborough was, but perhaps it was founded using astrological elections calculated by Pellitus. Edwinsborough certainly was an auspicious place, for it remains a major city, the capital of Scotland, Edinburgh.

Cadwallon transported his forces to Brittany in readiness for another attempted landing back in Britain. He was told there that Pellitus was Edwin's adviser and was clearly responsible for Edwin's advantage. So he decided to have Pellitus assassinated and sent one of his men, Brian, to York. By chance, in a York street, Brian met his sister, who had been taken from Worcester as a slave when that city was sacked by Edwin. She told him how to recognize Pellitus. Brian, in the clothing of a foreigner, waited until Pellitus was giving charity to the beggars who had assembled outside the gate of the king's residence. He joined the throng of beggars, and then he struck the astrologer with an iron staff he had had made especially for that purpose, and Pellitus was killed. Then Brian threw his staff away and melted into the crowd, evading capture.

Brian escaped and went to Exeter and sent a message to Cadwallon in Brittany. Meanwhile Penda, the pagan king of Mercia, hearing about the imminent return of Cadwallon, sent his Mercian forces southward and besieged Exeter. But the Mercians were repulsed when Cadwallon's army arrived from Brittany. Penda was forced to swear allegiance to Cadwallon and joined with his forces. The allies' army of Mercian pagans and Celtic Christians marched to Northumbria and took on Edwin. Edwin met them in battle at Heathfield, and without the advice of Pellitus suffered defeat. Edwin died in battle. His head was cut off and taken to York, where it was buried in the minster. Before the allied army arrived at York, Edwin's queen, Ethelburga, and the archbishop, Paulinus, fled by ship to Kent, taking with them the royal and ecclesiastical treasure. Northumbria was then ravaged by the victorious allies in a yearlong rampage, during which Edwin's successors, Osric and Eanfrid, were slain.

RAVENLANDEYE AND THE
RITUAL SUICIDE OF EARL SIWARD

In 1054 the *jarl* of Northumbria, Siward, surnamed Dirga, "the Valiant," at the head of an army of Anglo-Saxons and Danes, crossed the River Tweed into Northumbrian territory then under Scottish control. The invasion was in support of Malcolm, son of Duncan, who claimed the throne of Scotland occupied by Macbeth. Macbeth's army was worsted, though Siward's son Oshirn fell in the battle, in which around forty-five hundred men died. Macbeth was slain three years later in 1057 at Bothgowan.

In the battle, Siward's standard-bearer carried the magic flag, Ravenlandeye. According to William of Ramsay, writing in *The Crowland Chronicle* in the twelfth century, Siward acquired this luck-flag while riding along the rocky Northumbrian coast when he was

Fig. 12.1. Saint
Mary's Church, York,
where Ravenlandeye
was kept

stopped by an old cloaked and hooded man. The old man took out a raven banner, called Ravenlandeye, from his cloak and gave it to the jarl. Of course the old man, whoever he was, was in the typical guise of Woden, as the raven is his tutelary bird. Siward, in an age when the old religion had been absorbed by the newer, donated the banner to the church as a magical protector of the city of York. This pagan luck-flag hung in Saint Mary's Church for many years.

Raven banners were consecrated luck-flags of Viking warriors, and each banner, when magically empowered and carrying both the literal and symbolic meanings of the rune Wyn, was given a name. One of the most famous raven banners was Land-Waster, the standard of the Norwegian king Harald Hardrada. This was made by the daughters of the great Viking Ragnar Lodbrog and was carried from Norway to Constantinople and back in the campaigns of the Varangian Guardsmen. Finally, at the Battle of Stamford Bridge in 1066, the banner's luck ran out when Harald Hardrada was defeated by the English army under Harold II Godwinson. In the same year William of Normandy won the Battle of Hastings under two luck-flags, his own banner, Gonfanon, and another specially consecrated by the pope for the conquest of England.

By then Siward Dirga was dead, having died in 1055. Dying of what was probably dysentery, he ordered his men to dress him in his armor and carry him with his ax and shield to the highest point of the walls of York. There, he edged himself off his bed and fell over the edge of the wall to his death. The nineteenth-century artist's impression (see figure 12.2, opposite) shows a Christian priest administering the last rites. But Siward's death was not approved by the church, for it was the ritual suicide of a warrior in accordance with the Elder Faith. Siward said that he would die like a man, not an animal on straw, and he did. The raven banner called Ravenlandeye was deposited in Saint Mary's Church in York after Siwald's death. This was not the first time that a pagan sacred artifact ended up adding to the sanctity of a church.

Fig. 12.2. Death of Jarl Siward

OTHER SACRED BANNERS OF NORTHUMBRIA

Another important luck-flag was kept in the collegiate church of Saint John the Evangelist at Beverley, a most holy place where lawbreakers could claim sanctuary. It was taken in to battle on two occasions. This was the banner of Saint John of Beverley. In the year 937, on his way to fight at Brunanburgh, King Æthelstan left his sword on the altar of Beverley Minster in exchange for the banner of Saint John of Beverley. Larwulf carried it into battle, and the king's army prevailed over his enemies.

In 1138, King David of Scotland invaded England with an army composed of Scots, Picts, and men from several other nations who rallied to his call. "Multitudes uncalled for allied themselves" as the chronicler Richard of Hexham wrote, "either from love of plunder, or opportunity of revenge, or the mere desire of mischief with which that region was rife.

Overrunning the province, and sparing none, they ravaged with sword and fire almost all Northumberland as far as the river Tyne . . . laying waste in the same way the greater part of the territory of Saint Cuthbert on the west side." The war crimes committed by this army outraged even the brutal standards of the twelfth century. The barons of the province came together at York to decide how to counter the invasion.

Then Turstin, archbishop of York, declared a holy war against the invaders, as in addition to murder, rape, and pillage they were looting and burning churches as they went. As it was now a crusade, the church brought together three of the sacred luck-flags of Northumbria for use in battle magic. Richard of Hexham tells us, "They therefore hastened to resist them; and passing the village of Alverton [Northallerton], they arrived early in the morning at a plain distant from it about two miles. Some of them soon erected, in the center of a frame, which they brought, the mast of a ship, to which they gave the name of the Standard. . . . On the top of this pole they hung a silver pyx containing the Host, and the banner of Saint Peter the Apostle, and John of Beverley and Wilfrid of Ripon, confessors and bishops."

The banner of John of Beverley had carried the power of Wyn for the winning side 201 years earlier at the Battle of Brunanburgh. Setting up the standard was a unique magical act, bringing together magically effective totems designed to disempower the enemy and empower the defenders of Northumbria.

As the army of the king of Scotland "advanced in this order to battle, the standard with its banners became visible at no great distance; and at once the hearts of the king and his followers were overpowered by extreme terror and consternation; yet, persisting in their wickedness, they pressed on to accomplish their bad ends." But the standard had its magical effect. "Between the first and third hours, the struggle of this battle was begun and finished. For numberless Picts being slain immediately on the first attack, the rest, throwing down their arms, disgracefully fled. The plain was strewed with corpses; very many were taken prisoners; the king and all the others took to flight; and at length, of that immense army all were either slain, captured, or scattered as sheep without a shepherd."

Eight hundred years later the battle flag of Yorkshire, a white rose on a black pennant, was attached to a spear and carried by a standard-bearer under fire during the D-Day Normandy landings of 1944. Thus the power of Wyn and Gar prevailed. The flag is preserved in the regimental museum in York, the same city where Ravenlandeye was hung in Saint Mary's Church.

THE MAGIC OF LORD SOULIS

The story of Lord Soulis is a Northumbrian legend that contains many elements of traditional magic, and a ballad composed by John Leyden put the legend of Lord Soulis of Hermitage Castle into a literary form. Hermitage Castle was a key fortress in the borderlands of England and Scotland, a border that moved many times over the centuries before being stabilized along its present line. According to local tradition Soulis was a practitioner of magic who was a cruel and treacherous tyrant who oppressed his vassals and slaves as much as his enemies. Soulis had a familiar sprite called Old Redcap. Redcap made Soulis magically woundproof so he could not be harmed by edged weapons; neither could he be bound by chain or rope, but only by sand, which cannot be made into ropes.

> *While thou shalt live a charmed life,*
> *And hold that life of me,*
> *'Gainst lance and arrow, sword and knife,*
> *I shall thy warrant be.*
>
> *Nor forged steel, nor hempen band,*
> *Shall e'er thy limbs confine,*
> *Till threefold ropes of twisted sand*
> *Around thy body twine.*

Fig. 12.3. Lord Soulis

Being woundproof against edged weapons is part of the Northern Tradition magical repertoire. In 1031, Tore the Hound, leader of the pagan peasants who rose up against the persecuting Christian King Olaf of Norway at the Battle of Stiklastad, wore a magic reindeer-skin coat made for him by a Saami shaman. It rendered him woundproof. Because of this he was able to fight his way through and slay the king.

Soulis's enemies went to the king of Scotland, and after they repeatedly complained to the king about Soulis, the king told them, "Boil him if you please, but let me hear no more of him." So they ambushed Soulis, but their weapons would not bite. Nevertheless they succeeded in forcing him to the ground with spears. But when they bound him with ropes, the ropes broke. Then they used chains, and these too would not hold. Then they tried magic ropes. Sand was taken from the stream called Nine Stane Burn. Nine handfuls of barley chaff were added and threefold ropes made from it. This is a form of binding magic that is reminiscent of threshold pattern making under the aegis of the rune Nyd. This means of binding Lord Soulis was discovered by Thomas the Rhymer, who had been in the otherworld with the queen of Elfland. True Thomas instructed that the ropes of sand should be contained inside tubes of lead, and it was these with which Soulis was bound. Then, wrapped in leaden bonds that disempowered his magic, he was boiled to death in a cauldron. They brought a brass cauldron and set it on a fire at Nine Stane Rigg, which is the ridge separating Liddesdale and Teviotdale, on the top of which stands a megalithic circle of nine stones. Then Soulis was boiled to death in the cauldron inside the circle.

> *On a circle of stones they placed the pot,*
> *On a circle of stones but barely nine;*
> *They heated it red and fiery hot,*
> *Till the burnished brass did glimmer and shine.*
>
> *They rolled him up in a sheet of lead,*
> *A sheet of lead for a funeral pall;*
> *They plunged him in the cauldron red,*
> *And melted him, lead, bones and all.*
>
> *At the Shelf-hill, the cauldron still*
> *The men of Liddesdale can show;*
> *And on the spot, where they boil'd the pot,*
> *The spreat and deer hair ne'er shall grow.*

DIVINE KINGSHIP AND ROYAL SAINTS

Sainthood in the Christian Church was the continuation of the apotheosis of the pagan kings, couched in language taken from the new religion. Traditionally the Anglo-Saxon kings were held to have a special relationship with the gods, in the case of the Angles, through their ancestral descent from Woden, and thereby to possess the innate power of maegen. Most Anglo-Saxon saints are members of royal dynasties, thereby of Wodenic descent. Death by violence, especially in battle, was enough to guarantee veneration. The maegen of royal personages was transferred to the place where the death happened and to artifacts associated with the person at the time of death. Frequently, the chroniclers tell us, the moment of death and the place where it happened were marked by supernatural happenings, apparitions, and miracles. For example, after King Æfwald of Northumbria was murdered by Sicga in the year 789, *The Anglo-Saxon Chronicle* tells us that "a heavenly light was often seen at the place where he was killed."

The Christian Church continued the pagan practice of keeping up sacred days of the gods by making new ones dedicated to their saints. So the saints of Old Northumbria all have their days on which they are remembered. King Osric of Deira (father of Oswin), who had reverted to his pagan beliefs before his death in battle in the year 634, was nevertheless commemorated as a saint for May 8 in an early eighth-century calendar. After his death he was erased from the list of kings because of his reversion to the Elder Faith but later was reinstated, perhaps because he was venerated anyway. Osric died at the hands of the Celtic Christian king of the Welsh, Cadwallon.

Several less contentious Northumbrian saints had festivals in the Christian calendar that were celebrated all over England. Some remain today, despite the wholesale removal of saints by Catholic and Protestant alike. The earliest Northumbrian saint of the year is commemorated on January 7, which is the holy day of Cedd, who died in the year 664. He was sent from the holy island of Lindisfarne as a missionary to the Anglians in the kingdom of Mercia, and afterward went to Essex and became bishop of the East Saxons in London. Finally Cedd returned to Northumbria, where he founded the monastic cell of Lastingham, where his bones were later enshrined in a special crypt as part of the cult of relics. January 12 is holy to Biscop Baducing, a Northumbrian nobleman known under his monkish name, Saint Benedict Biscop. He was the founder of the Wearmouth and Jarrow Monasteries, and he lived circa 628–690. Biscop was an importer of ideas and techniques from mainland Europe, and he brought to Northumbria various artistic and architectural techniques as well as the cult of relics.

March 2 is Saint Chad's Day. Chad was Cedd's youngest brother. Like him, he trained at Lindisfarne and became abbot of Lastingham and then archbishop of York. He was expelled from York in the year 669 and went to Lichfield in Mercia. The cathedral there is dedicated to him. Chad died of the plague in 672. Bede, a famed monk of Jarrow, was fêted on May 27. He was known for writing several notable books, including *The Ecclesiastical History of the English People,* which was completed in the year 731. It is from this work of Bede that much of Northumbrian history is known, though it is biased, condemning acts of violence by pagan kings that were praised when Christian kings committed the same acts. Bede considered King Ecgfrith cursed, though he was venerated as a saint for having died in battle. In 1899, Bede was made a saint by the Roman Catholic Church, so Catholics call him Saint Bede, while Protestants know him as the Venerable Bede.

August 9 is the holy day of King Oswald (604–642). King of Northumbria, he was killed in the Battle of Maserfield (modern Oswestry) during a military incursion into Mercia. The Mercians, led by the staunchly pagan King Penda, dismembered Oswald's corpse and set his body parts on posts near a holy well as an offering to Woden. These were later recovered by his Christian followers, and a healing cult was set up at the well after the death of Penda. On August 20 the church commemorated the day of Oswini, a cousin of King Oswald, who was murdered on the orders of King Oswiu at Gilling in Yorkshire in the year 651. August 31 is the day of Saint Aidan, a Scots-Irish monk from Iona, who at the request of King Oswald was sent as a missionary to Northumbria. He founded the monastery on the holy island of Lindisfarne, though he was buried in Lincolnshire. Aidan died in 651.

October 25 is the holy day of Saint John of Beverley (died 721). Archbishop of York, he retired to his own foundation at Beverley

Minster, Yorkshire, the great sanctuary with the friðstool, a stone chair in which a fugitive criminal could sit and be granted permission to leave England for exile in Scotland or mainland Europe. The luck-flag called the banner of Saint John of Beverley was carried by the standard-bearer of King Æthelstan at the Battle of Brunanburgh in 937 and again on a wagon leading the army of the archbishop of York in his holy war against the Scots at the Battle of the Standard at Northallerton.

Although Christianity in Northumbria had been founded by members of the Celtic Church, it was the place where that church came under attack from the Catholic Church and where the seeds of its destruction were sown. In the year 663 a church synod was held at Whitby to standardize the calculation of the date of Easter in the Celtic and Catholic Churches in Northumbria. Until then different systems had been used, and the two churches celebrated Easter Sunday in different weeks. The Catholic faction under Wilfred overrode Bishop Colman's defense of the Celtic method on the grounds of standardization, and the Roman Easter was subsequently enforced. This spelled the beginning of the end of the Celtic Church, for many of the Celtic monks then withdrew back to their home monasteries, allowing the archbishop of Canterbury, Theodore, to call the Council of Hertford in 672, which effectively set up a church organization for the whole of England. Celtic priests had come largely from families of hereditary guardians of holy places of the Elder Faith. The Orthodox Church, of which the Roman Church was still a part, depended on central authority that did not have its roots in local communities. Northumbria was at the meeting point between these two rival interpretations of the Christian religion, and there the decentralized, nonhierarchical system lost out to the better-organized, centralist, hierarchical one.

SAINTS IN THE CULT OF BONES

Because the old ways were part of everyday life, repeated church laws against the practice of the Elder Faith were largely ineffective. This was especially true in the countryside, which has always been more difficult to police than towns. Pagan sacred artifacts could easily be passed off as Christian ones or hidden, to be brought out only to keep up the day. Non-Christian sacred and magical objects were, and still are, hidden away in hidey-holes, brought out only at the right time, handed down in the family, and only shown to trusted people. For those who could write there were times when it was too dangerous to write anything down, lest the writings were found by inquisitors and the owner tortured and killed, so many of these traditions were handed down only by word of mouth, until the present day. Yet despite all these attempts to wipe out indigenous culture there, embedded within the Christian Church is the cult of ancestors that existed in European society before the church existed. This is manifested in the cult of bones, where, after the innovations of Saint Benedict Biscop, every church in Northumbria needed to have "relics" of saints kept in it somewhere to authorize its spiritual existence; that is, human remains of people considered by the church to be in some way worthy. Consecration rites of churches included bringing in these skulls or bones, or occasionally mummified hearts, bottles of blood, or fabrics stained with the blood of the saint, and enshrining them in an altar or reliquary.

The crypt at Lastingham, a monastery founded by Cedd in the year 660, is a place where his bones were displayed for pilgrims to worship. Such churches had special undercrofts, houses of the dead, which were built specifically to hold and exhibit the saints' bones to the faithful. At Lastingham, Cedd took over a pagan holy place, praying and fasting to drive out the spirits dwelling there. Legend tells that he had twenty-nine followers who came with him to Lastingham. Twenty-eight died there of the plague, while the survivor was the only one who had *not* been baptized. Cedd died at Lastingham in the year 664. Later the church was destroyed by Danish pagans in the ninth century, but subsequently it was rebuilt. The present crypt, dating from the year 1080, is built into the hillside. A similar crypt at Ripon enshrined the bones of Wilfred, who died in the year 670.

In Northumbrian history we have a remarkable instance of the cult of bones in the story of Saint Cuthbert, long after his death. Cuthbert, bishop of Lindisfarne, died in March 687. He was buried at Lindisfarne, but in 698, for some reason, it was decided to dig him up from his stone sarcophagus and put him in a wooden coffin. In the year 875 the inhabitants of the monastery fled "the wicked army of the unbelievers," a Danish military incursion from their base in Repton. The monks took away not only their books, ritual paraphernalia, and treasure but also the remains of Cuthbert. Bishop Eardulph and his monks traveled around northern Northumbria for seven years. Many of the churches dedicated to Saint Cuthbert in that region are clearly places where the traveling monks stopped with his bones. Saint Cuthbert's Well at Bellingham may also be a stopping place in his bones' journey through the land. The area is known generally as the Territory of Saint Cuthbert.

This ritual perambulation of the northlands seems to have been first to Elsdon and down the River Rede to Haydon Bridge, then up the South Tyne to Beltinghame, then along the road by Hadrian's Wall to Bewcastle. From there they turned south to Salkeld and via Eden Hall and Plumbland into Lancashire and the River Derwent. Here they attempted to cross to Ireland, but the ship was caught up in a storm, and they were forced to return to the port from where they had embarked. Then they went northward to Whithorn, on the Galloway coast, then southward again across Stainmoor into Teesdale. From Cotherstone the trail runs through Marske, Forcett, and Barton to Craike Abbey near Easingwold. They and Cuthbert's bones stayed there four months before they resumed their travels, going to Chester-le-Street. The monastery was refounded there, Cuthbert was reburied, and Chester-le-Street became the seat of the bishop of Bernicia.

In the year 995, Bishop Aldhun removed Cuthbert's bones to Ripon, but in 997 the monks took the bones away from there and moved on. The place where the bones should have been was located by an *ostentum* (an unexpected but meaningful happening) when the monks carrying the bones came to a place called Wardenlawe. There, when they came to pick the coffin up again, they found that they could not move it anymore. Then the bishop and his monks fasted and prayed for three days for inspiration for what to do next. It was revealed to Eadmer, "a virtuous man," that the bones should be taken to Dunholme, a holy island. But the monks did not know the country and had no idea where Dunholme was. They decided to go onward until they came across someone who knew. They overheard a woman looking for her cow, who asked another woman if she had seen it. The second woman answered that the cow was at Dunholme. The monks went with her to find the cow, and there they built a church as the repository of the much-traveled bones.

A Germanic pre-Christian tradition of reconsecrating land considered desecrated by perambulating the land while carrying sacred objects is related to this perambulation of the north by the monks of Lindisfarne. After a failed attempt by Christian missionaries to impose their religion on a pagan country, ritual reconsecration of the profaned land was carried out by the Goths then inhabiting the Black Sea region. Images of the gods were carried on camels throughout the country, with appropriate rites and ceremonies conducted at the sacred places the Goths visited. The Christian monks of Northumbria appear to have been carrying around the bones of Cuthbert in a similar attempt to reconsecrate the land ravaged by the pagan Danes. Sanctified stopping places on trackways had been originated long before the Christian religion, and in the seventh century the Northumbrian monk Ovin from Lastingham traveled along these trackways, setting up crosses at stopping places where formerly there would have been waystones.

The holy ground of Durham Cathedral was reputed to have power against serpents. A local tale is told that in the year 1060 or thereabouts a man called Osulf went to sleep in a field and woke to find a serpent coiled around his neck. He pulled it off and threw it to the ground, but it forced its way back onto him, and whatever he did, Osulf found it impossible to stop the snake from getting back around his neck. He threw it on a fire, but it did not burn and was back again. Then he cut it to pieces with a sword, but the pieces reassembled and his burden continued. When he entered Durham Cathedral the snake fell off and remained outside. But when he came out, it got back around his neck. Finally he stayed inside the cathedral for three days, fasting and praying, and when he finally emerged the serpent had gone.

The Sockburn Worm, "a monstrous poisonous vermin, wyvern, ask or werme" that plagued a place called Graystone on the banks of the River Tees was slain by Sir John Conyers using a magic weapon called the Conyers Falchion, kept at Durham Cathedral. This edged weapon is connected with a ritual conducted when a new Durham bishop makes his first entry into the city. The rite took place in the middle of Neasham Ford or, if the Tees was in flood, on Croft Bridge. The bishop was offered the Conyers Falchion with this speech: "My lord bishop, I here present you with the Falchion wherewith the champion Conyers slew the worm, dragon, or fiery flying serpent which destroyed man, woman, and child; in memory of which the king then reigning gave him the manor of Sockburn, that upon the first entrance of every bishop into the county this Falchion should be presented."

13
YR

The Outlaw Archers

THREE OF THE NORTHUMBRIAN RUNES are related to the yew tree (*Taxus baccata*), the tree of life and death: the thirteenth rune, Eoh, the fifteenth, Eolh-Secg, and the twenty-seventh rune, Yr. All three runes are defensive in character. *The Old English Rune Poem* adage for Eoh reads: "On the outside, Yew is a rough tree, but strong and firm, the fire's guardian upheld by deep roots, a joy to the household." This shows yew not only as the pothook but also as the strong and firm, defensive wood of the bow; as this poem says, "The bow is a joy to princes and noblemen, a sign of value, looks good on horseback, fast in its course, a fine tool." The area of the old kingdom of Northumbria had the most famous archers of medieval times. The legendary archer outlaws Adam Bell, Clym of the Clough, William of Cloudesly, and Robin Hood are famed in old ballads. Because Robin Hood is most famous, many of the stories told of the northern outlaws, resembling in their elements the Norse sagas, are also told of him. While Robin Hood and his Merry Men frequented the forests of Sherwood and Barnsdale on the southern edge of old Northumbria, Adam Bell, Clym of the Clough, and William of Cloudesly lived in the forest of Englewood, near Carlisle. The name Englewood denotes the wood of Ing, wood for making fires. There is a connection with

Robin Hood, for these three lived in the time of his father, who was also a champion archer.

> *The father of Robin a Forrester was,*
> *And he shot a lusty longbow*
> *Two north-country miles and an inch at a shot,*
> *As the Pindar of Wakefield does know:*
> *For he brought Adam Bell, and Clim of the Clough,*
> *And William of Clowdéslie*
> *To shoot with our Forrester for forty mark;*
> *And our Forrester beat them all three.*

The story begins with an account of how the three companion archers were outlawed for hunting deer. Discovered with the king's deer they fled to Englewood. But, unlike the others, William was married with a wife and family and returned to his village to visit them. Then he was betrayed by an old wife to the sheriff and the justice in nearby Carlisle. The sheriff's men surrounded his house and demanded he surrender to them. He refused, and the family retreated into an upstairs room together, William with sword and buckler in hands, defending his three children. His wife, Alyce, took up a poleax, the best weapon for fighting indoors, to defend the door. William then began to shoot at his assailants. One hit the justice, but his armor deflected the arrow and broke it into three. After this the sheriff ordered the house to be set on fire, to burn them all inside.

William's wife and children escaped from an upper window by climbing down sheets and avoided the sheriff's men, who were intent on killing or capturing William. Meanwhile William shot arrows at his assailants until the flames of the burning house became so hot that his bowstring burned and broke in two. William decided not to die a coward's death in the burning house but to come out fighting. This is the Northern Tradition custom of one deciding how to die and taking the brave and honorable option, like Earl Siward did when he committed ritual suicide. With his sword and buckler, William charged at his enemies, but they finally overcame him by throwing window shutters and doors on him. He was taken prisoner and led to Carlisle, where the sheriff condemned him to death immediately and ordered the master of the Guild of Carpenters to make a new pair of gallows on which to hang him. He ordered the gates of Carlisle shut so that none might come and rescue William of Cloudesly.

The next morning the journeymen carpenters were setting up the new gallows next to the pillory in the marketplace. A little boy asked the workmen, "What means that gallows tree?" and they told him the good yeoman William of Cloudesly was to be hanged there later that day. Though the town-wall gates were shut that morning, the boy managed to squeeze through a crevice in the wall and went to see Adam Bell and Clym of the Clough in the greenwood. He told them that their comrade was to hang that morning. They hastened to Carlisle and found the gates barred to all. Clym called to the gatekeeper and told him that he was in possession of the king's seal, meaning he was on royal business, and the porter foolishly opened the gate to them. The outlaws immediately fell on the gatekeeper and throttled him, taking his keys.

And now will we our bowes bend,
Into the towne will we go,
For to deliver our dear brother,
That lieth in care and woe.
Then they bent their good yew bowes,
And looked their stringes were rounde.

They entered the marketplace and there saw Cloudesly in a cart, bound hand and foot and with a strong rope around his neck, ready to be hanged. The justice called a lad to him to take Cloudesly's clothes, from which the sexton could take his measure to dig his grave. Cloudesly, given his customary right to say his last words on the scaffold, announced defiantly, "He who makes a grave for another may yet lie in it himself." Adam Bell and Clym of the Clough then took the initiative. Simultaneously they loosed their arrows. Adam's struck the sheriff, and Clym's the justice. Both fell, mortally wounded, and the onlookers fled. They untied Cloudesly, who wrested a battleax from an officer of the town, using it to cut down those who tried to rearrest him. The town hornblower blew the outhorn as a general alarm, and the mayor came at them with a poleax. But he too was killed. Cloudesly's comrades used their bows until they had run out of arrows, then fought with swords. Somehow they got to the gate and escaped into the greenwood.

> *When they came to Englyshe Wood*
> *Under the trusty tree,*
> *There they found bowes full good,*
> *And arrows in great plenty.*

By chance, back in Engelwood, Cloudesly was reunited with his wife and family, and he told them that he had gotten out yesterday "by sweet Saint John," referring to Saint John of Beverley, patron of escapees from justice. The outlaws decided to go to the king to ask for pardon and traveled south to London. Alyce and the children came with them. There they came to the royal court and entered the hall. The porter asked them who they were, and they told him they were outlaws. They were allowed to see the king and begged his pardon for killing the king's own deer. He asked their names and, when told, said they were notorious outlaws who deserved to be hanged. The king ordered them arrested, but his queen spoke up and asked for a boon, that they should be allowed to go free. The king agreed not to hang them, and they were given food and drink. But then he was handed a letter that told him that as well as killing his deer the outlaws also had killed the sheriff, justice, and mayor of Carlisle, almost all the constables, catchpoles, bailiffs, and beadles as well as many others, three hundred and more in all.

He ordered his best archers to come with him to the butts, where they would test these outlaw archers' abilities. The royal archers were not very good and kept missing the mark. Then the king asked Cloudesly what would he like to shoot at, and they set up two hazel rods twenty score paces apart.

> *"I hold him an archer," said Cloudesly,*
> *"that yonder wand cleveth in two."*
> *"There is none such," said the king,*
> *"Nor no man can so do."*

Cloudesly shot from the first wand and split the distant hazel wand in two. The king was astonished. Then Cloudesly said that he would perform an even greater feat. He ordered his seven-year-old son tied to a stake and an apple put on his head. Then from six score paces he would split the apple in two. The king said that if he should fail to do as he said, he should be hanged. Cloudesly drove a stake into the ground and tied his son to it, telling the boy to keep perfectly still and turn his head aside so he would not start when the arrow was loosed. Then from six score paces away, Cloudesly called for the spectators to be still, drew back the bow, and loosed the arrow. The arrow cleaved the apple, and the king said, "God forbid that you should shoot at me." Then the king took Cloudesly into his household as chief archer, and his comrades were made yeomen of the chamber in the king's bodyguard.

> *Thus endeth the lives of these good yeomen;*
> *God send the eternal bliss;*
> *And all, that with a handbow shooteth,*
> *That of heaven may never miss.*

The other great northern outlaw archer is the much more famous Robin Hood. He is indelibly associated with Sherwood Forest, which in medieval times measured twenty-five miles from north to south and ten miles across. All that remains today of Sherwood are the

Fig. 13.1. Robin Hood and his Merry Men

Dukeries, five connected country estates, set up in the seventeenth and eighteenth centuries when the land was taken over by the Dukes of Kingston, Newcastle, Norfolk, and Portland. But of course that was long after the era of Robin Hood. Robin Hood is also connected with Barnsdale Forest, in South Yorkshire. This area was much smaller than Sherwood, about five miles across, south of the River Went to the villages of Hampole and Skelbrooke, north of Doncaster. Wherever the action of the Robin Hood stories is located, many of the feats ascribed to William of Cloudesly are also ascribed to Robin Hood. History does repeat itself, as do stories.

The Old English Rune Poem tells of the Yr rune as a weapon that displays the skills of craftsmanship. This is the perfect combination of skills and knowledge applied to materials provided by nature, and archery involves the skills of bow- and arrow-making as well as the technique of shooting and being on target. As well as being a death-bringer, the bow can be used for divination, as in this old ballad of Robin Hood's last day alive. Here he shot a last arrow to divine where his grave should be. The ballad is titled "Robin Hood's Death and Burial," showing how he was taken ill and how he went to his cousin at Kirkley Hall, who performed bloodletting on him, which was the cause of his death.

When Robin Hood and Little John
Went over yon bank of broom,
Said Robin Hood to Little John,
"We have shot for many a pound.

"But I am not able to shoot one shot more,
My arrows will not flee;
But I have a cousin lives down below,
Please God, she will bleed me."

Now Robin is to fair Kirkley gone,
As fast as he cou'd wen;
But before he came there, as we do hear,
He was taken very ill.

And when that he came to fair Kirkley hall,
He knocked at the ring,
But none was so ready as his cousin herself
For to let bold Robin in.

"Will you please to sit down, cousin Robin," she said,
"And drink some beer with me?"
"No, I will neither eat nor drink,
Till I blood letted be."

"Well, I have a room, cousin Robin," she said,
"Which you did never see,
And if you please to walk therein,
You blood shall letted be."

She took him by the lily white hand,
And let him into a private room,
And there she blooded bold Robin Hood,
Whilst one drop of blood would run.

She blooded him in the vein of the arm,
And lock'd him up in a room;
There did he bleed all the livelong day,
Until the next day at noon.

He then bethought him of a casement door,
Thinking for to be gone;
He was so weak he could not leap,
Nor he could not get down.

He then bethought him of his bugle horn,
Which hung low down to his knee;
He set his horn unto his mouth,
And blew out strong blasts three.

Then Little John, when hearing him,
As he sat under the tree,
"I fear my master is near dead,
He blows so wearily."

Then Little John to fair Kirkley is gone,
As fast as he could dree;
But when he came to Kirkley hall,
He broke locks two or three;

Until he came bold Robin to,
Then he fell on his knee;
"A boon, a boon;" cries Little John,

"Master, I beg of thee."

"What is that boon," quoth Robin Hood,
"Little John, thou begs of me?"
"It is to burn fair Kirkley hall,
And all their nunnery."

"I ne'er hurt fair maid in all my time,
Nor at my end shall it be;
But give me my bent bow in my hand,
And my broad arrows I'll let flee.

"And where this arrow is taken up,
There shall my grave digged be.
With verdant sods most neatly put,
Sweet as the green wood tree."

"And lay my bent bow by my side,
Which was my music sweet,
And make my grave of gravel and green,
Which is most right and meet."

"Let me have length and breadth enough,
With a green sod under my head;
That they may say, when I am dead,
Here lies bold Robin Hood."

"But take me upon thy backe, Little John,
And beare me to yonder streete,
And there make me a full fayre grave,
Of gravell and of greete."

"And sett my bright sword at my head,

Mine arrowes at my feete,
And lay my yew bow by my side,
My met-yard wi."

These words they readily granted him,
Which did bold Robin please;
And there they buried bold Robin Hood,
Near to the fair Kirkleys.

Kirkleys was beautiful of old,
Like Winifrid's of Wales,
By whose fair well strange cures are told
In legendary tales.

Upon his grave was laid a stone,
Declaring that he dy'd,
And tho' so many years ago,
Time can't his actions hide.

Thus he that fear'd neither bow nor spear
Was murder'd by letting blood;
And so, loving friends, the story ends,
Of valiant bold Robin Hood.

There is nothing remains but his epitaph now,
Which, reader, here you have,
To this very day, which read you may,
As it was upon the grave:

Robert Earl of Huntington
Lies underneath this little stone.
No archer was like him so good:
His wildness nam'd him Robin Hood.

Full thirteen years, and something more,
These northern parts he vexed sore.
Such outlaws as he and his men
May England never know again!

The legends of William of Cloudesly and Robin Hood have had many interpretations over the years: romantic, folkloristic, political, pagan, and ecological. The outlaws in the greenwood have been linked to the old pagan gods, members of the Wild Hunt, participants in the rites and ceremonies of May Day, Anglo-Saxon resistance against Norman power, or peasants fighting for their freedom from oppressive overlords; they have become the inspiration for back-to-nature movements and those who champion rural values against the onslaught of industrial urbanism. Today in Sherwood Forest postcards are on sale depicting Robin Hood as ecological guardian of the ancient oaks that grow there. Like the best of legends, each successive generation can find a new interpretation suitable for the time. That is how legendary figures like William of Cloudesly and Robin Hood remain timeless.

Fig. 13.2.
The grave of
Robin Hood

14

OTHERWORLDLY BEINGS OF THE NORTHUMBRIAN LANDSCAPE

Boggarts, Hobs, Brownies, and Bogeymen

OLD NORTHUMBRIA IS KNOWN FOR its numerous kinds of otherworldly beings and beasts that frequent the landscape, farms, and dwellings. The Gabriel Ratchets of Northumbria are a form of the Wild Hunt led by Gabriel as the master of the hunt, doomed to ride forever through the sky, collecting human souls. Those who hear the yelping of the hounds, sounding like litters of puppies, have received a portent of approaching death. Hobs are the name for spirits who dwell in and guard the woodlands. The hobthrush is a kind of sprite who lives in holes in the moor or coastal caves such as Hob Hole near Runswick Bay in North Yorkshire. The barguest is literally a gate ghost who haunts gateways, crossings, ginnels, and other narrow places, including gorges among the rocks. Often it appears in the form of a black dog, called Trash or Skriker in Lancashire and Old Shuck or Black Shuck in East Anglia. Occasionally the apparition of a white cat or cow or even a headless man or woman is called a barguest. He or she who encounters a barguest has been given a warning of impending death. The cross on the Pennine High Point Cross Fell was set up to ward off the barguests, boggards, or boggarts who attacked wayfarers on the fells. Between Settle and Austwick is a small cave in which dwelled the Boggart of Cave Ha, which had the habit of leaping on the horses of people riding by. An old saying, "It comes and it goes like the Thorpe Hesley Boggard," refers to the random and recurring appearing and disappearing of boggarts; such activity is also seen from the evil, shape-shifting spirits called black weasels.

The bogglebo or bugaboo is another name given to a boggart, but shape-shifting witches also have been called by this name, as in the legend of Old Bogglebo, who made Jock the Keelman ferry her across the mouth of the River Wear to Sunderland in a storm. When they arrived a black cat leaped ashore, and the ferryman did not get paid his fare. The bogeyman is a related being, of course always male. He may be heard in the night making ominous noises, and during the Industrial Revolution he became a human bogieman, who, with his hammer, tested the soundness of bogie wheels of trains standing in the sidings at night. Old Bogey is also a nickname for the devil. When it was first introduced, many people referred to a dilly (that is, a steam locomotive) as Old Ned, its fire, smoke, and noise reminding them of the hellish attributes of the infernal spirit. Jack-in-Irons is another kind of bogeyman, haunting nighttime roads, clanking and clattering the chains in which he is fettered.

The demon called Old Scratch or Old Scrat is known across England, from East Anglia to Lancashire and up to the borderlands. An appearance of Old Scratch is as if a heavy load comes suddenly on something being carried or on a vehicle. The extra weight appears suddenly on a truck or van, in former years on a cart or wagon. This makes the engine or the horses pull very hard although the vehicle clearly has no load. In former times carters reported seeing Old Scratch as a small imp dancing between the horse's ears when this happened. Pallbearers taking a coffin to the graveyard sometimes reported this sprite's heavy effect, and priests used to banish him by name if such an event occurred.

There are ancient accounts of sacred wagons in ancient times suddenly becoming heavy when the god or goddess was present there, ready for his or her ritual perambulation of the area. The stories of Old Scratch recall the same phenomenon.

Houses must be protected against all manner of otherworldly beings, hence the many rites and ceremonies of building and of traditional built-in protective charms and sigils. The lubber fiends are hairy and unintelligent sprites who come to occupy the hearths of farmhouses, absorbing all the warmth and light of the fire. The Daeg mark on a speer post next to the inglenook is a means of keeping them away. The night-mare is an evil sprite who appears in the form of a dog or cat. A means of countering it is to put one's shoes under the bed with the toes pointing outward. In the region of Old Northumbria the brownies are benevolent house sprites who do small acts of kindness to the inhabitants. However they must be acknowledged with a bowl of milk. The dobbie-stanes that stand by farm gates are stones with a depression in them for feeding the brownies their milk, though most people when asked will tell one that the milk is for the cat. Preindustrial breweries always had such a stone, as the aid of a brownie in brewing good ale is essential. If a brownie is offended by ill treatment after being so helpful, it may change its character and transform into a house boggart or homesprite, a troublesome entity who carries out mad pranks aimed at the offending householder. The cunning men's tradition is to disempower these sprites by planting a tree by the infected house in whose roots they are entangled, and there they must stay so long as the tree lives.

IOR: THE WORMS OF NORTHUMBRIA

Many places in Northumbria have their own giant serpent and dragon legends, some of which have been retold in ballads and folksongs or in embellished form by creative writers. Stories are told of these beasts of old Northumbria at Bishop Auckland, Dunstanburgh, Durham, Handale, Kellington, Lindisfarne, Linton, Longwitton, Nunnington,

Slingsby, Sockburn, Spindleston Heugh, Tynemouth, Washington, Well, and Whorl Hill. Here are the most notable of these stories, retold in my words. As they are manifestations of the rune Ior, most of these Northumbrian beasts are called by the generic term *worm*. It is from the Old Norse word *ormr,* present in the North Wales serpentine headland the Great Orme. As a species the worm is variously described as a dragon, wyvern, asp, or fiery serpent. The English word *vermin* is related—an animal considered harmful that ought to be extirpated. Northumbrian worm stories are set in an early medieval period and contain many magical elements.

THE LAMBTON WORM

The Lambton Worm is the most famed and most written about of all the Northumbrian worms. The aristocratic Lambton family was noted for its bravery, fearing neither man nor god. The heir of Lambton, John, was fishing in the River Wear one Sunday, thereby breaking the day of rest. As he was having a bad day, catching nothing, he swore at passersby on their way to church. Then his luck changed, and his fishing line went taut, and he knew he had a large catch. It was. But when he eventually got his catch on land, it was not a fish but a weird worm. Angered, he tore it from the hook and threw it down a well, which, unusually, was by the riverbank. A local returning from church asked Lambton if he had caught anything, and he replied, "Why, truly, I think I've caught the devil," for it was something like a newt with nine holes on each side of its head. He told the woman to look down the well, and she replied, "No good will come of it."

But catching the worm was a shock to Lambton, and he became very religious and went away on a pilgrimage to Jerusalem. The worm grew in the well until the well was no longer large enough to contain it; then it burst out and took up residence in the middle of the River Wear, coiled around a large rock. At night it came on land, and as it grew it could coil around a small hill, making nine circuits in all. It ravaged the countryside for food, devouring sheep and sucking the milk from cows. Lord Lambton, the father of the angler who brought the worm out in the first place, thought it would be possible to appease the worm by filling a trough with the milk from nine cows in the hope that it would then go away. This plan backfired, and the worm came the next day for another helping of milk; when it got none it rampaged through the lordship, tearing up trees. Then they fed it, and it returned each day for more.

Lord Lambton offered a reward to any man-at-arms or knight who would kill the worm. Many tried, some were wounded or killed, and those who cut through the worm saw it regenerate before their eyes. Seven years this went on, and by then the farms of the region were depleted and the country was a wasteland with a hungry worm ready to attack anyone who came near. Then John Lambton finally returned from the Middle East, having been given up for dead. He decided to consult the famous wisewoman, Old Elspat of the Glen, as to his course of action. She told him that as he had been the cause of the disaster, only he could bring it to an end. She told him of a smith who could make him special armor covered with sharpened blades. Then he should stand on the worm's rock in the river and await its return. But to be successful he had to swear to the wisewoman that after killing the worm he would slay the first living thing he encountered as a thanksgiving sacrifice. If he failed to do this the Lambton family would be cursed for nine generations.

So the smith made the special armor, and before setting out to the river to encounter the worm, John Lambton asked his father to set loose his dog when he heard the hunting horn sound three blasts. The dog would run to him and then would be sacrificed. John Lambton went to the river and got across to the rock to await the worm. When it came the worm dodged Lambton's sword and coiled around him to constrict him to death. But the razor-sharp steel blades that studded the armor cut through the beast's coils, and gradually as it lost blood and the river ran red with it, the worm lost strength. Finally Lambton was freed from its grip, and he cut it in two with his sword. The pieces fell into the river, but the current separated them and they could not reunite. That was the end of the worm. John Lambton regained the riverbank and blew the hunting horn to signal that the worm was destroyed. Then his father ran to greet him, forgetting to loose the dog first. Of course John could not kill his father as a sacrifice, so the curse of the worm fell on the Lambton family for nine generations.

There are several surviving ballads and Tyneside dialect songs about the Lambton Worm. The following one was written for a pantomime performed at the Old Tyne Theatre in Newcastle in 1867.

One Sunday morning Lambton went a-fishing in the Wear:
And catched a fish upon his hook he thought lenk't very queer.
But whatt'n a kind of fish it was young Lambton couldn't tell.
He wanted fish to carry home, so he hoyed it in a well.

Whisht' lads, hold your gobs, and I'll tell you all an awful story,
Whisht' lads, hold your gobs, and I'll tell you all about the worm.

Now Lambton felt inclined to gan, and fight in foreign wars,
He joined a troop of knights that cared for neither wounds nor
*   scars,*
And off he went to Palestine where queer things him befell,
And very soon forgot about the queer worm in the well.

Whisht' lads, hold your gobs, and I'll tell you all an awful story,
Whisht' lads, hold your gobs, and I'll tell you all about the worm.

But the worm got fat and growed and growed, and growed an
*   awful size,*
With great big teeth and great big gob, and great big googly eyes.
And when at nights he crawled about to pick up bits o' news,
If he felt dry upon the road, he milked a dozen cows.

* * *

Whisht' lads, hold your gobs, and I'll tell you all an awful story,
Whisht' lads, hold your gobs, and I'll tell you all about the
worm.

This fearful worm would often feed on calves and lambs and
sheep,
And swallow little bairns alive when they laid down to sleep.
And when he'd eaten all the cud and he had had his fill,
He crawled away and lapped his tail ten times round Pensher
Hill.

Whisht' lads, hold your gobs, and I'll tell you all an awful story,
Whisht' lads, hold your gobs, and I'll tell you all about the worm.

The news of this most awful worm and his queer gannins on,
Soon crossed the seas and got to the ears of brave and bold Sir
John.
So home he came and catched the beast and cut him in two halves,
And that soon stopped his eating bairns and sheep and lambs and
calves.

Whisht' lads, hold your gobs, and I'll tell you all an awful story,
Whisht' lads, hold your gobs, and I'll tell you all about the worm.

So now you know how all the folks on both sides of the Wear
Lost lots of sheep and lots of sleep and lived in mortal fear.
So let's have one to brave Sir John that kept the bairns frae
harm,
Saved cows and calves by making halves of the famous Lambton
Worm.

Now, lads, I'll hold my gob, that's all as knows about the story
Of Sir John's clever job with the awful Lambton Worm.

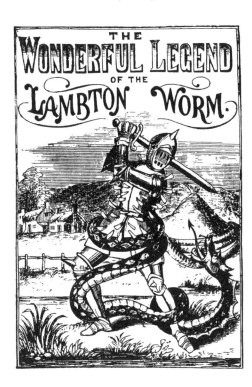

Fig. 14.1. Cover of a pantomime program, 1875

Worm Hill is still there, in the parish of North Biddick, close to the River Wear. Worm Well was close by and was resorted to ceremonially at Midsummer Eve as a wishing well. Sometime after 1840 the well was destroyed, but in the 1970s a new well was made as a tourist attraction. But because Washington Development Corporation deemed the real well to be too close to the river's edge, for "health and safety" reasons the replica well was built on another site, farther from the Wear, and water was supplied to it by a pipe.

THE LAIDLEY WORM
OF SPINDLESTON HEUGH

The legend of the Laidley or Loathly Worm is an old story recalled in the song "The Laidley Worm of Spindleston Heugh," supposedly written by Duncan Frazier, "the Old Mountain Bard" of Cheviot, about the year 1270. The story is located at Bamburgh, Northumberland, once the capital of Bernicia, founded by King Ida in the year 548. This worm legend is directly connected with the founder's family. Ida had two children: a daughter, Margaret, and a boy who succeeded him historically, called Ethelric, but in this tale he is called the Child of the Wynde. When he was grown the son went to the ancestral lands in Angeln and was not seen for many years. Ida's queen died, and he married another woman, who, unknown to him, possessed magical powers. She saw Margaret as her rival and put a curse on her, transforming her into a horrible dragon, the Laidley Worm. From being a beautiful young woman, she became a repulsive monster; an old Northumbrian expression is "as ugly as the Laidley Worm." Margaret, now in the shape of the Laidley Worm, fled the castle and went to Spindleston Heugh on the River Waren, where she coiled herself around a rock in her new life as a dragon. Like all worms, she needed prodigious amounts of food and began to lay waste to the surrounding land. To appease her, each day the locals filled a trough with the milk of seven cows for her to drink.

Childe Wynd thrice kisses the
Laidly Worm & rescues his Sister
the Princess Margaret.

Fig. 14.2. The
Laidley Worm

Eventually the Child of the Wynde was told what had happened to his sister. He and his thirty-three kinsmen had a ship of rowan built, and they sailed in it to Northumbria. It was made of rowan, whose wood is powerful against bewitchment, so that the evil queen's magic had no power to sink it. The worm however, not knowing who was on board and seeing it as a threat, attempted to wreck the ship. The ship was beached in Budle Bay, and the Child of the Wynde ran to Spindleston Heugh to combat the beast. But as he attacked, the worm spoke in a soft voice that he recognized as his sister's, asking him to spare her. When he realized the true identity of the worm he kissed its brow. The worm then went into a cave. A moment later, from the cave emerged his sister, for the kiss had dispelled the curse. They went immediately to the castle, where there was rejoicing, except for the queen, whose magic had been undone by the Child of the Wynde. The spell being broken and the evil queen's magic being neutralized, her own curse then fell on her, and she was immediately transmuted into a toad who went to live in a cave under the castle, appearing occasionally to terrify young women.

THE SOCKBURN WORM

Another Northumbrian worm was at Sockburn, which lies in a meander of the River Tees. Like the other beasts, it terrorized and laid waste to the locality, so someone had to do something to end it. Attempts were made to appease the worm with troughs of milk, as in the Lambton case, but this proved futile. The man chosen to kill the worm was the local knight, Sir John Conyers. According to *Bowes's Manuscript,* which preserves the story, the knight "slew that monstrous and poisonous vermin, wyvern, ask or werme, which had overthrown and devoured many people in fight: for that the scent of the poison was so strong that no person might abyde it. And by the providence of the Almighty God, the said John Conyers, Knight, overthrew the said monster and slew it. . . . That place where this great serpent lay was called Graystone, and this John lyeth buried in Sockburne church." Like John Lambton, Sir John Conyers wore a suit of armor studded with razor-sharp blades. The magic weapon Conyers used was the Conyers Falchion, a type of sword with a broad blade two and a half feet in length. It dates from the thirteenth century and is still in existence. The cross of the Falchion bears images of dragons with foliated tails. This weapon was the title deed of the manor, playing its part in a ritual when the lord of the manor met each new bishop of Durham at his entry into the diocese.

THE WODE WORM OF LINTON

Linton, ten miles from Jedburgh, is the locus of the Wode Worm legend. The place-name bears the element *lind,* which is associated with this kind of beast, as in the dragon called Lindwurm who lives in German-speaking lands. Also the word *wode,* as in the god Woden, can signify rage or divine frenzy. At Linton the Worm's Hole was its lair, and during the day, it coiled around Wormington Hill nearby. By means of its breath the worm drew flocks and herds to it, which it then devoured. As was usual, various champions attempted to destroy the worm, to no avail. Finally the Laird of Larriston decided to take on the beast. As the worm was immune to conventional medieval weaponry, the laird dipped a piece of peat in pitch, put it on the end of a lance, and set fire to it. He then rammed it down the worm's throat. The fumes from the burning pitch both obliterated the worm's noxious breath and suffocated the worm. As it died it tightened its coils on Wormington Hill, making the spiral pattern still visible there. An effigy in Linton church records the deed.

> *The wode laird of Larristone*
> *Slew the Worme of Wormestone*
> *And was a Linton Parochine.*

THE LONGWITTON DRAGON

Sir Guy of Warwick is famed for slaying Colbronde, the Danish champion, and the monstrous Dun Cow of Dunsmore Heath. The Dun Cow is likely to have been an aurochs, the tameless wild cattle, the living embodiment of primeval strength expressed in the rune Ur. He also killed a dragon who had the power to make itself invisible. It lived in the oak wood at Longwitton in Northumberland, a grove that contains three holy wells known collectively as Our Lady's Wells. Thomas Percy's *Reliques of Ancient English Poetry* contains "The Legend of Sir Guy," an ancient story mentioned by Geoffrey Chaucer.

> *On Dunsmore Heath I also slewe*
> *A monstrous wylde and cruell beast,*
> *Calld the Dun-cow of Dunsmore Heath;*
> *Which many people had oppressed . . .*

> *A dragon in Northumberland*
> *I alsoe did in fight destroye,*
> *Which did bothe man and beast oppresse,*
> *And all the countrye sore annoyed.*

THE NUNNINGTON DRAGON

On the River Rye near Helmsley in the parish of Stonegrave lived the Nunnington Dragon. Its lair was in a wooded place called Loschy Hill, from whence it emerged to devour livestock and destroy crops. A knight called Peter Loschy agreed to kill the dragon, so he had an armorer make a suit of armor studded all over with razor-sharp blades. Accompanied by his hound, Loschy went to fight the dragon. Upon encountering the knight the dragon coiled around him, but the blades sorely wounded the beast and it retreated, only to return, because its wounds had healed in an instant. The dragon, like the

Lambton Worm, had the power of regeneration, for as soon as a part was cut off it reconnected itself, and the dragon was whole again. The combat resumed, and with his sword, Loschy was able to cut off part of the dragon. The dog immediately seized the piece and carried it off to a hill about a mile away. As Loschy gradually cut up the dragon, so the dog carried off each piece to the hill. Finally only the head was left. But then, in triumph, they went too close to the dragon's jaws. Both knight and dog were poisoned and fell dead.

THE DRAGONS OF TYNEMOUTH PRIORY

A chamber carved in the rock on which Tynemouth Priory was built was made for the Northumbrian King Ceolwulf. The ballad "The Wizard's Cave" recounts how Walter, son of Robert the Knight, went in search of treasure in this cave. But although there were dragons guarding the cavern, the story is somewhat of an anticlimax, for he entered and found the treasure.

> *Fierce dragons with scales of bright burnished brass*
> *Stand belching red fire where the warrior must pass.*
> *But rushes on he with his brand and his shield,*
> *And with loud shrieks of laughter they vanish and yield.*

The cave, called Jingling Geordie's Hole, was blocked later.

THE WORM OF WELL

Eight miles north of Ripon is the village of Well, the place of a holy well dedicated to Saint Michael. Here a knight called Latimer fought and killed the worm in the usual fashion. In the vicinity are several places with stone carvings of the coat of arms of the Latimer family, showing a dragon.

YORKSHIRE DRAGONS

Most of the Yorkshire dragon tales are basic stories of dragonslaying with common motifs. The Wantley Dragon of Wharnciffe Chase, in Yorkshire, near "fair Rotherham" is recounted in a ballad of 1685 preserved, like Sir Guy's story, in Thomas Percy's *Reliques of Ancient English Poetry*. At Wantley the dragonslayer was More of More Hall.

> *Some say this dragon was a witch,*
> *Some say he was a Devil,*
> *For from his nose a smoke arose,*
> *And with it burning snivel;*
> *Which he cast off, when he did cough,*
> *In a well that he did stand by;*
> *Which made it look just like a brook,*
> *Running with burning brandy.*
>
> *More of More Hall*
> *Did engage to hew the dragon down;*
> *But first he went, new armor to*
> *Bespeak at Sheffield town;*
> *With spikes all about, not within but without;*
> *Of steel so sharp and strong;*
> *Both behind and before, arms, legs, and all o'er,*
> *Some five or six inches long.*

Clad in spiky armor like that worn by Lambton and Loschy, More overcame the dragon after a battle lasting two days and a night. It was written, "It is not strength that always wins, for wit doth strength excel."

At Handale lived the Serpent of Handale, who lurked in Scaw Wood and ate young maidens. It was slain by a youth called Scaw, who liberated an earl's daughter, held captive by the serpent in a cave, and was richly rewarded for it. Near Hutton Rudby, also in Yorkshire, lived a dragon who coiled around the mound called Sexhowe. The locals appeased its appetite by providing the milk of nine cows each day. A passing knight killed the dragon, then departed, leaving its carcass on a hilltop. It was skinned, and the skin was hung up as a relic in the church at Stokesley. At Kellington on the River Aire near Pontefract in Yorkshire a dragon was slain by Armroyd the shepherd, using his crook as a weapon. As in the Nunnington legend, both man and dog died of dragon venom once it was slain. In the church is the Kellington Serpent Stone, a grave slab carved with a cross and a serpent.

POSTSCRIPT

ANCESTRAL TREASURES

LIKE THE ELDRITCH DWELLERS who exist embedded unnoticed in the landscape, only to reappear without warning to the unwary, the runes have never gone away. Since their inception there is no time until the present day when someone has not been using them at some place. In England, because they had been used on Northumbrian Christian monuments, the runes were never classified as witchcraft, which happened in Iceland, leading to official killings of rune users. When they were no longer used officially as writing the runes continued to be carved by almanac makers on the wooden calendars known as primestaves or clog almanacs. They were carved, painted, and stamped as craftsmen's and merchants' marks on various artifacts and as good-luck or apotropaic glyphs wherever appropriate.

During the Renaissance all of the known ancient alphabets of Europe were collected together by scholars such as Athanasius Kircher. Books and prints were published detailing them, and they found their way into murals in palaces and Catholic monasteries in mainland Europe. The Northumbrian runes also survived on stone monuments such as the Bewcastle, Ruthwell, and Thornhill Crosses and in a number of Anglo-Saxon manuscripts preserved in private libraries in England and mainland Europe. One of the Cotton manuscripts

143

Fig. P.1. A clog
almanac

(*Codex Otho BX*), unfortunately destroyed in a fire in 1731, had the
thirty-three Northumbrian runes written in it. Fortunately, by the time
this tenth-century manuscript was destroyed, the Northumbrian runes
had been published by G. Hickes in 1705 in his *Linguarum Veterum
Septentrionalium Thesaurus*.

These runes were seen as important ancestral treasures, and
when Viscount Cobham decided to build the Temple of Liberty
in the landscaped grounds of the grand country house at Stowe in

Fig. P.2. *Sunna*, sculpture by John Michael Rysbrack

Buckinghamshire, the Northumbrian runes became part of the ensem-
ble. Built as a symbol of the inalienable English freedoms, the temple's
design was commissioned from James Gibbs, master of sacred geometry
and architect of the fine London churches of Saint Martin-in-the-Fields
and Saint Mary-le-Strand. Built between 1744 and 1748, the Temple
of Liberty is a triangular building in the Gothic style with pentagonal
towers at the three corners. Around the temple were set marble sculp-
tures of seven Saxon gods: Sunna, Mona, Tiw, Woden, Thuner, Friga,
and Seatern, corresponding to the astrological planets. These had been
made earlier by the sculptor John Michael Rysbrack. Their names are
carved in Northumbrian runes. There was also a sevenfold altar to
these ancestral gods.

The Temple of Liberty was designed to embody what its makers called the Saxon tradition, from which we have our traditional English liberties. These are trial by jury, a right granted by King Alfred at a moot at Stonehenge; the human rights enshrined in the Magna Carta, including habeas corpus, the right not to be imprisoned arbitrarily without charge and fair trial; and the right of representation in Parliament. The Temple of Liberty is dedicated appropriately "To the Liberty of Our Ancestors," and the runes carved on the gods' plinths reflect this ancient right. It is from these ancient times that our traditional rights come, and it is up to us to defend them in the face of those who would take them from us.

Fig. P.3. The Temple of Liberty

GLOSSARY

Agrimensor: Member of the Roman guild of surveyors who used the spiritual principles of the Disciplina Etrusca, the Etruscan Discipline.

Aibitír: The Gaelic alphabet.

Airt: One of the eight directions, a family, one of the divisions of eight runes.

Bautasteinar: Uninscribed standing stones denoting a *vé* (q.v.).

Bootless: A person declared bootless became an outlaw (q.v.).

Corn: The traditional Scottish ceremonial drinking cup, made from an aurochs' horn with a lip of chased silver.

Corridor of Sanctity: The alignment of seven sacred places in the city of York.

Crann-gafainn: The poisonous herb henbane, used in borderlands magic associated with the rune Is.

Curragh: Traditional boat made of a wooden framework covered by waterproofed animal hides.

Cryptic runes: Encryption is part of the ancient runemasters' repertoire. Forms include the Iis runes (numbers of individual strokes), the branch runes (*kvistrünar*), the tree runes (*hahalruna*), and the tent runes (*tjaldrünar*).

Derilan: Divinely inspired guardian of a holy well.

Dilly: The original name for a steam locomotive, a word from Wylam

Colliery, where the first practicable steam locomotives worked.

Dobbie-stone (dobbie-stane): Flat stone with a depression in it for holding liquids.

Elder Faith: The polytheistic, Earth-venerating, ancestral religion of the peoples of northern Europe.

Enhazeled: Area of land divided off from the everyday world and sanctified by the erection of hazel posts around it.

Frithman: A person who had claimed sanctuary but who could never go outside the *leuga* (q.v.) of Beverley.

Friðstool: Sacred seat of peace that guaranteed sanctuary for fugitives from justice.

Futhark: The older rune rows that begin with the runes *F, U, Th, A, R, K.*

Futhork: The thirty-three-character Northumbrian rune row that begins with *F, U, Th, O, R, K.*

Gansey: Fisherman's sweater, knitted with symbolic and magical local glyphs and patterns.

Geomancy: The ancient European art of placement. The Etruscan Discipline is the most systematized form of geomancy from the first millennium BCE.

Hällristningar: Scandinavian rock art of the late Bronze Age and the transition to the Iron Age (ca. 1300–800 BCE).

Hof: Banqueting hall used in the Elder Faith for sacred meals, such as the Yuletide feast.

Hogrune: Rune associated with the powers of the mind.

Irminsul: "The universal pillar," a sacred post that represented the world axis, which stood in the Saxon pagan sanctuary at Ober-Marsberg, Germany.

Jarl: The rank of earl.

Leuga (baneluca): Sacred boundary around a sanctuary.

Lindwurm: Dragon-serpent associated with the linden tree (*Tilia platyphyllos*) in German-speaking countries. (See Worm.)

Luck-flag: A sacred banner carried in battle as the personal standard of a lord or king.

Maegen: A personal force, distinct from physical strength or political power, the possession of which assures success and good fortune.

Mete-wand: A measuring stick.

Metod: Destiny, doom, and death.

Nornir or Norns: The three fates, personified as the Weird Sisters, in the Northern Tradition.

Ostentum: An unexpected but meaningful happening.

Outhorn: Town horn used to raise a general alarm, the forerunner of the mechanical siren.

Outlaw: A person declared beyond the protection of the law. It was the duty of every law-abiding person to kill an outlaw if at all possible.

Port: A lively tune played on the bagpipes.

Raven Banner: Luck-flags bearing the emblem of the raven were used by the Vikings in battle.

Relic: A fragment of human body, such as a skull, bones, or blood from a person regarded as holy. These objects were enshrined as objects of worship in churches, a continuation of the cult of ancestors of the Elder Faith.

Stafgarðr: Sacred enclosure fenced with hazel posts.

Stance: Place where drovers' cattle could stop and graze overnight, marked with a clump of Scots pines.

Stave: Both the runic characters themselves and the wooden staves on which they are cut, as runestaves are cut on a runestaff.

Tiver: The red pigment of madder (*Rubia tinctorum*), used magically to color runes.

Tjosnur: Ritual pegs carved with human heads, used to peg down to the ground a hide used in ritual single combat.

Valknute, Valknut, or Valknútr: A glyph of three interlaced equilateral triangles, associated with the god Woden/Odin as "the knot of the slain."

Vardlokkur: The magical technique of warding and binding, exemplified in the rune Haegl.

Vé: A Northern Tradition sacred enclosure in the shape of a triangle or *v*.

Vébond: A fence around a *vé*.

Warlock: A man with the power of binding spirits.

Web of Wyrd: The interwoven fabric of things, places, events, actions, and persons that make up our world as we experience it.

Wih: An unsheltered, outdoor image of a deity.

Wode: Divine frenzy, an attribute of the god Woden.

Worm: A Northumbrian word for a dragon or outsized serpent.

Woundproof: Having magical protection that prevents one from being wounded or killed by an edged metal weapon.

Wyrd: That which comes to happen.

BIBLIOGRAPHY

Andrews, William. *Bygone Durham*. London: W. Andrews & Co., 1898.

Anonymous. *Jerseys Old & New*. St. Helier: n.p., n.d.

Appadurai, Arjun. *Modernity at Large*. Minneapolis: University of Minnesota Press, 1997.

———. *The Social Life of Things: Commodities in Cultural Perspective*. Chicago: Cambridge University Press, 1988.

Arnold, Christopher J. *The Archaeology of the Anglo-Saxon Kingdoms*. London: Routledge, 1997.

Arntz, Helmut. *Handbuch der Runenkunde*. Haale, Germany: Max Niemeyer, 1944.

Aspelin, J. H., Haye Hamkens, Siegfried Sieber, and Friedrich Mössinger. *Trojaburgen*. Translated by Michael Behrend and Debbie Saward. Thundersley and Bar Hill, England: The Caerdroia Project, 1982.

Aswynn, Freya. *Leaves of Yggdrasil*. Saint Paul, Minn.: Llewellyn Publications, 1994.

Ayres, James. *British Folk Art*. London: Barrie & Jenkins, 1977.

Bächtold-Stäubli, Hanns, ed. *Handwörterbuch des deutschen Aberglaubens*. 9 vols. Berlin: Walter De Gruyter, 1927–1942.

Backhouse, Janet. *The Lindisfarne Gospels*. Oxford: Phaidon Press, 1987.

Baetke, Walter. *Das Heilige im Germanischen*. Tübingen, Germany: Mohr, 1942.

Banks, M. M. "Tangled Thread Mazes." *Folk-Lore* 46 (1935): 78–80.

Bass, Joseph A. *Famous Trees of Robin Hood's Forest*. Newark, England: Albatross Publishing, 1999.

Bateson, Gregory. *Steps to an Ecology of Mind*. New York: Chandler Publications, 1972.

Bauman, Zygmunt. *Modernity and Ambivalence*. Ithaca, N.Y.: Cornell University Press, 1988.

Bebbington, David. *Patterns in History*. Leicester, England: Inter-Varsity Press, 1979.

Bernard, Julian. *The Decorative Tradition*. London: Architectural Press, 1973.

Bianchi, Udo. *Selected Essays on Gnosticism, Dualism and Mysteriosophy*. Leiden, the Netherlands: Brill, 1978.

Bilfinger, Gustav. *Zeitrechnung der alten Germanen*. Stuttgart, Germany: C. Liebich, 1901.

Birch, Lionel, ed. *The History of the T.U.C. 1868–1968*. London: Trades Union Congress, 1968.

Blachetta, Walther. *Das Buch der Deutscher Sinnzeichen*. Berlin: Widukind Verlag, 1941.

Blakeborough, Richard. *Wit, Character, Folk-Lore and Customs of the North Riding of Yorkshire*. London: Henry Frowde, 1898.

Bossert, Helmut T. *Folk Art of Europe*. London: A. Zwemmer, 1954.

Branston, Brian. *The Gods of the North*. London: Thames & Hudson, 1955.

Braudel, Fernand. *The Structures of Everyday Life*. Translated by Siân Reynolds. New York: Harper & Row, 1981.

Brears, Peter. *Horse Brasses*. Feltham, England: Country Life Books, 1981.

———. *North Country Folk Art*. Edinburgh: John Donald Publishers, Ltd., 1989.

Brett, David. *On Decoration*. Cambridge: Lutterworth Press, 1992.

Bringéus, Nils-Arvid, ed. *Arbete och redskap*. Stockholm: Carlsson, 1988.

Broadwood, Lucy, and E. Fuller Maitland. *English County Songs*. London: Leadenhall Press, 1893.

Brockie, William. *Legends and Superstitions of the County of Durham*. London: Sunderland, 1886.

Brown, Roger John. *English Farmhouses*. London: Robert Hale, Ltd., 1982.

Brunskill, Ronald W. *Illustrated Handbook of Vernacular Architecture*. London: Faber & Faber, 1987.

Bryce, Derek. *Symbolism of the Celtic Cross*. Felinfach, Wales: Llanerch Enterprises, 1989.

Bucke, Richard Maurice. *Cosmic Consciousness: A Study in the Evolution of the Human Mind*. Philadelphia, Pa.: Innes & Sons, 1901.

Buckley, Joshua. "Keeping Up the Day. Joshua Buckley Interviews Nigel Pennick." *Rûna* 15–16 (2004): 2–5; 7–10.

Buschan, Georg. *Illustrierte Völkerkunde.* Stuttgart, Germany: Strecker und Schröder, 1926.

Carpenter, Edward. *The Art of Creation: Essays on the Self and Its Powers.* London: George Allen & Unwin, 1904.

Carrington, Noel, and Clarke Hutton. *Popular English Art.* London and New York: Penguin Books, 1945.

Carter, Jenny, and Janet Rae. *Traditional Crafts of Scotland.* Edinburgh: Chambers, 1988.

Chadwick, Hector Monro. *The Origin of the English Nation.* Cambridge: Cambridge University Press, 1907.

Chaney, William. *The Cult of Kingship in Anglo-Saxon England.* Manchester, England: Manchester University Press, 1970.

Chisholm, James Allen. *True Hearth: A Practical Guide to Traditional Householding.* Smithville, Tex.: Rûna-Raven Press, 1993.

Coatsworth, Elizabeth, and Michael Pinder. *The Art of the Anglo-Saxon Goldsmith.* Woodbridge, England: Boydell Press, 2002.

Cockayne, Thomas Oswald. *Leechdoms, Wortcunning and Starcraft.* London: Longman, Roberts and Green, 1864.

Collingwood, William Gershom. *Northumbrian Crosses of the Pre-Norman Age.* London: Faber and Gwyer, 1927.

Cooper, Emmanuel. *People's Art: Working-Class Art from 1750 to the Present Day.* Edinburgh and London: Mainstream, 1994.

Corrsin, Stephen D. *Sword Dancing in Europe: A History.* Middlesex, England: Enfield Lock, 1997.

Cunningham, Allan. *Traditional Tales of English and Scottish Peasantry.* London: F. & W. Kerslake, 1874.

Cyr, Donald L., ed. *Full Measure.* Santa Barbara, Calif.: Stonehenge Viewpoint, 1990.

Dannheimer, Hermann, and Rupert Gebhand, eds. *Das keltische Jahrtausend.* Mainz, Germany: Von Zabern, 1993.

Danser, Simon. *The Myths of Reality.* Wymeswold, England: Alternative Albion, 2005.

Davidson, Hilda R. Ellis. "Hooded Men in Celtic and Germanic Tradition." In *Polytheistic Systems,* edited by Glenys Davies, 102–24. Edinburgh: Edinburgh University Press, 1989.

———. *The Lost Beliefs of Northern Europe.* London: Routledge, 1993.

Davídsson, Ólafur. "Isländische Zauberbücher und Zauberzeichen." *Zeitschrift des Vereines für Volkskunde* 13 (1903): 150–67.

De Benoist, Alain. *On Being a Pagan*. Atlanta, Ga.: Ultra, 2004.

Deneke, Bernwald. *Europäische Volkskunst*. Frankfurt, Germany: Main/Wein, 1980.

Denyer, Susan. *Traditional Buildings and Life in the Lake District*. London: Gollancz, 1991.

Devall, William, and George Sessions. *Deep Ecology: Living as if Nature Mattered*. Salt Lake City, Utah: Peregrine Smith Books, 1985.

Dickens, Bruce. *Runic and Heroic Poems*. Cambridge: Cambridge University Press, 1915.

Dickinson, William Croft. *Scotland from the Earliest Times to 1603*. Oxford: Clarendon, 1977.

Dietrichson, Lorenz. *De Norske stavkirker, studier over deres system, oprindelske og historiske udvikling*. Christiania, Denmark: Cammermeyer, 1892.

Dobson, Richard Barry, and John Taylor. *Rymes of Robin Hood*: *An Introduction to the English Outlaw*. London: Stroud, 1997.

Dodwell, Charles Reginald. *Anglo-Saxon Art: A New Perspective*. Manchester, England: Manchester University Press, 1982.

Douglas, Mary. *Implicit Meaning*. London: Routledge & Kegan Paul, 1975.

Drake-Carnell, Francis John. *Old English Customs and Ceremonies*. London: Batsford Ltd., 1938.

Düwel, Klaus. *Runenkunde*. Stuttgart, Germany: J. B. Metzlersche Verlagsbuchhandlung, 1968.

Eco, Umberto. *Travels in Hyperreality*. Translated by William Weaver. London: Jovanovich Publishers, 1986.

Edwards, Gillian. *Hobgoblin and Sweet Puck*. London: Bles, 1974.

Elliot, Ralph W. V. *Runes: An Introduction*. Manchester, England: Manchester University Press, 1959.

Endell, August. "Originalität und Tradition." *Deutsche Kunst und Dekoration* 9 (1901–1902): 289–96.

Enright, Michael J. "The Goddess Who Weaves." *Frühmittelalterliche Studien* 24, (1990): 54–70.

Evans, Angela Care. *The Sutton Hoo Ship Burial*. London: British Museum Publications, 1986.

Falconer, Alan. *Rambler's Riding*. London: Robert Hale, 1975.

Farwerk, Frans Eduard. *Noordeuropese mysterien*. Deventer, the Netherlands: Ankh-Hermes, 1970.

Fevre, Ralph W. *The Demoralization of Western Culture: Social Theory and the*

Dilemmas of Modern Living. London and New York: Continuum, 2000.

Filipetti, Hervé, and Janine Troterau. *Symboles et pratiques rituelles dans la maison traditionelle.* Paris: Berger Levrault, 1978.

Fisher, Douglas John Vivian. *The Anglo-Saxon Age.* London: Longman Press, 1973.

Flowers, Stephen E. *Runes and Magic: Formulaic Elements in the Older Runic Tradition.* Bern: Lang, 1986.

Frampton, Kenneth. "Toward a Critical Regionalism." In *Postmodern Culture,* edited by Hal Foster. London: Pluto Press, 1985.

Franklin, Anna. *Hearth Witch.* Earl Shilton, England: Lear Books, 2005.

———. *The Illustrated Encyclopaedia of Fairies.* London: Vega Books, 2002.

Gaitzsch, Wolfgang. *Antike Korb- und Seilerwaren.* Aalen, Germany: Limesmuseum, 1986.

Garrard, Bruce, and David Rossiter. *The Arrow: The Founding of the New Cathedral at Salisbury.* Salisbury, Wiltshire, England: n.p., 1980.

Garrigan, Kristine O. *Ruskin in Architecture: His Thought and Influence.* Madison: University of Wisconsin Press, 1973.

Giddens, Anthony. *Modernity and Self-Identity.* Redwood City, Calif.: Stanford University Press, 1991.

Gorman, John. *Banner Bright: An Illustrated History of Trade Union Banners.* Buckhurst Hill, England: Scorpion Press, 1986.

Graham, Frank. *The Castle and Walls of Newcastle.* Newcastle upon Tyne, England: Northern History Booklets, 1972.

Green, Dennis Howard. *Language and History in the Early Germanic World.* Cambridge: Cambridge University Press, 1998.

Greeves, Lydia, and John Miller. *Country Cottages.* London: Pavilion Books, 1995.

Grimm, Jakob. *Deutsche Mythologie.* Berlin: F. Dümmler, 1875.

Gundarsson, Kvedúlfr Hagan. *Our Troth.* Seattle, Wash.: Vikar, 1993.

Hammarstedt, Nils Edvard. *Svensk forntro och folksed.* Stockholm: Nordiska Museet, 1920.

Hanson, Richard Patrick Crosland. "The Transformation of Pagan Temples into Churches in the Early Christian Centuries." In *Studies in Christian Antiquity,* edited by Richard Patrick Crosland Hanson. Edinburgh: T. & T. Clark, 1985.

Hartley, Marie, and Joan Ingilby. *The Old Hand-Knitters of the Dales.* Otley, England: Smith Settle, 2001.

Harvey, Michael, and Rae Compton. *Fisherman Knitting.* Princes Risborough, England: Shire Publications, 1978.

Heggie, Douglas C. *Megalithic Science.* London: Thames & Hudson, 1981.

Henderson, William. *Notes on the Folk-Lore of the Northern Counties of England and the Borders.* London: Folk-Lore Society, 1866.

Herbert, Kathleen. *Looking for the Lost Gods of England.* Hockwold-cum-Wilton, England: Anglo-Saxon Books, 1994.

Herrmann, H. A. "Mühle und Donnerbesen." *Germanien* 10 (1942): 333.

Hillgarth, Jocelyn N. *Christianity and Paganism, 300–750: The Conversion of Western Europe.* Philadelphia, Pa.: University of Pennsylvania Press, 1986.

Holm, Charles, ed. *Old English Country Cottages.* London & New York: The Folklore Society, 1906.

Howlett, David. "Inscriptions and Design of the Ruthwell Cross." In *The Ruthwell Cross,* edited by Brendan Cassidy. Princeton, N.J.: Princeton University Press, 1992.

Hutchinson, John, and Anthony D. Smith, eds. *Ethnicity.* Oxford: Blackwell, 1996.

Jeffri, Joan, ed. *The Craftsperson Speaks.* Westport, Conn.: Greenwood Publishing Group, 1992.

Jekyll, Gertrude. *Old West Surrey.* London: Longmans, Green, & Company, 1904.

Jensen, K. Frank. *Magiske runer.* Copenhagen: Sphinx, 1991.

Jones, Francis. *The Holy Wells of Wales.* Cardiff: University of Wales, 1954.

Jones, Graham. *Saints in the Landscape.* London: Stroud, Tempus, 2007.

Jones, Prudence. *A "House" System from Viking Europe.* Cambridge: Cambridge University Press, 1991.

———. *Northern Myths of the Constellations.* Cambridge: Cambridge University Press, 1991.

———. *Sundial and Compass Rose: Eight-fold Time Division in Northern Europe.* Bar Hill, England: Fenris-Wolf, 1982.

Jones, Prudence, and Nigel Pennick. *A History of Pagan Europe.* London: Routledge, 1995.

Jones, Sidney. *The Village Homes of England.* London: Batsford Ltd., 1912.

Knight, Richard Payne. *The Symbolical Language of Ancient Art and Mythology: An Enquiry.* New York: J. W. Bouton, 1876.

Koch, Rudolf. *The Book of Signs.* London: The Limited Editions Club, 1930.

Kostof, Spiro. *A History of Architecture: Settings and Rituals.* Oxford: Oxford University Press, 1985.

Lämmle, August. *Brauch und Sitte in Bauerntum.* Berlin: De Gruyter, 1935.

Larson, Katherine. *The Woven Coverlets of Norway.* Seattle: University of Washington Press, 2001.

Lauweriks, Johannes Ludovicus Mattheus. *De ladder van het zijn.* Bussum, the Netherlands: n.p., 1904.

Leahy, Kevin. *Anglo-Saxon Crafts.* Stroud, England: Tempus, 2003.

Leighton, Henry R. *Memorials of Old Durham.* London: George Allen & Sons, 1910.

Lerner, Daniel. *The Passing of Traditional Society.* Glencoe, Ill.: Free Press, 1958.

Lethaby, William Richard. *Architecture, Mysticism and Myth.* London: Percival, 1891.

———. "Art and Workmanship." *The Imprint* 1 (1913): 1–3.

Lorenz, Konrad. *The Waning of Humaneness.* Translated by Robert Warren Kickert. London: Unwin Hyman, 1989.

Lundqvist, Sune. "Hednatemplet i Uppsala." *Förnvannen* 18 (1923): 85–118.

Lyle, Emily B. *Archaic Cosmos: Polarity, Space and Time.* Edinburgh: Polygon, 1990.

MacKail, John William. *The Life of William Morris.* 2 vols. London: Longmans, Green & Company, 1899.

Mackie, John Duncan. *A History of Scotland.* Harmondsworth, England: Penguin, 1964.

Macleod, Fiona. *The Winged Destiny: Studies in the Spiritual History of the Gael.* London: Heinemann, 1910.

Mair, Craig. *Mercat Cross and Tolbooth.* Edinburgh: John Donald Publishers, 1988.

Mannhardt, Wilhelm. *Wald- und Feldkulte.* Berlin: Gebrüder Borntraeger, 1877.

Massingham, Harold John. *The English Countryman: A Study of the English Tradition.* London: Batsford Ltd., 1942.

———. *Fee, Fi, Fo, Fum: The Giants in England.* London: K. Paul, Trench, & Trubner, 1926.

Mattil, Edward. *Meaning in Craft.* Englewood Cliffs, N.J.: Prentice Hall, 1965.

McFadzean, Patrick. *Astrological Geomancy: An Introduction.* Limited edition of 40. York, England: Northern Earth Mysteries, 1985.

McNeill, F. Marian. *The Silver Bough*. 4 vols. Glasgow, Scotland: William Maclellan, 1957–1968.

Messenger, Betty. *Picking up the Linen Threads: A Study in Industrial Folklore*. Austin: University of Texas Press, 1978.

Michell, John. *The John Michell Reader: Confessions of a Radical Traditionalist*. Rochester, Vt.: Inner Traditions, 2005.

Morris, William, et al. *Arts and Crafts Essays*. London: Rivington, Percival & Company, 1893.

Naylor, Peter, and Lindsey Porter. *Well Dressing*. Ashbourne, England: Landmark Publishing, 2002.

Neumann, Erich. *The Origins and History of Consciousness*. Translated by R. F. C. Hull. Bollingen Series XLVII. New York and London: Princeton University Press, 1954.

Nikolaysen, Nicolay. *The Viking Ship from Gokstad*. Christiania, Denmark: A. Cammermeyer, 1882.

Nioradze, Georg. *Der Schamanismus bei den sibirischen Völkern*. Stuttgart, Germany: Strecker und Schröder, 1925.

Norbury, James. *Traditional Knitting Patterns from Scandinavia, the British Isles, France, Italy and Other European Countries*. New York: Dover Publications, 1973.

Ogilvie, Elizabeth, and Audrey Sleightholme. *An Illustrated Guide to the Crosses on the North Yorkshire Moors*. Thorganby, England: Village Green Press, 1994.

Olsen, Olaf. *Hørg, hof og kirke*. Copenhagen: Gad, 1966.

Ord, John Walker. *The History and Antiquities of Cleveland*. London: Simpkin and Marshall, 1846.

Oyama, Susan. *The Ontology of Information*. Cambridge, Mass.: MIT Press, 1985.

Page, Raymond Ian. *An Introduction to English Runes*. London: Methuen, 1973.

Parker, C. A. "Knitting-Sticks." *Transactions of the Cumberland and Westmorland Antiquarian Society* NS XVII (1917): 88–97.

Parkinson, Thomas, Rev. *Yorkshire Legends and Traditions*. 2 vols. London: E. Stock, 1888, 1889.

Paulsen, Peter, and Helga Schach-Dörges. *Holzhandwerk der Alamannen*. Stuttgart, Germany: Kohlhammer, 1972.

Pearson, Michael. *Traditional Knitting: Aran, Fair Isle and Fisher Ganseys*. London: William Collins Sons & Company, 1984.

Peesch, Reinhard. *The Ornament in European Folk Art.* New York: Alpine Fine Arts Collection, 1983.

Pennick, Nigel. *The Ancient Science of Geomancy.* London: Thames & Hudson, 1979.

———. *Anima Loci.* Cambridge: Electric Traction Publications, 1993.

———. *Beginnings: Geomancy, Builders' Rites and Electional Astrology in the European Tradition.* Chieveley, England: Capall Bann Publishing, 1999.

———. *Caerdroia: Ancient Turf, Stone and Pavement Mazes.* Trumpington, England: Megalithic Visions Etcetera, 1974.

———. *Celtic Art in the Northern Tradition.* Bar Hill, England: Fenris-Wolf, 1991.

———. *The Celtic Cross: An Illustrated History and Celebration.* London: Blandford, 1997.

———. *Celtic Sacred Landscapes.* London: Thames & Hudson, 1996.

———. *The Celtic Saints.* London: Godsfield Press Ltd., 1997.

———. *The Complete Illustrated Guide to Runes.* Shaftesbury, England: Element Books, 1999.

———. *The Cosmic Axis.* Bar Hill, England: Fenris-Wolf, 1985.

———. *Crossing the Borderlines: Guising, Masking and Ritual Animal Disguises in the European Tradition.* Chieveley, England: Capall Bann Publishing, 1998.

———. *Daddy Witch and Old Mother Redcap: Survivals of the Old Craft under Victorian Christendom.* Bar Hill, England: Fenris-Wolf, 1980.

———. *Das runen Orakel.* Munich, Germany: Karl Friedrich Hörner, 1990.

———. *Earth Harmony.* London: Century, 1987.

———. *Einst war uns die Erde heilig.* Waldeck-Dehringhausen, Germany: Felicitas-Hübner, 1987.

———. *The Eldritch World.* Earl Shilton, England: Lear Books, 2006.

———. *Games of the Gods.* London: Ebury Publishing, 1989.

———. "Geomancy." *The Other Britain.* Supplement to *Cambridge Voice,* 1970, 16.

———. *Holy Sepulchre: The Round Churches of Britain.* Trumpington, England: Megalithic Visions Etcetera, 1974.

———. *The Inner Mysteries of the Goths: Rune-lore and Secret Wisdom of the Northern Tradition.* Chieveley, England: Capall Bann Publishing, 1995.

———. *Labyrinths: Their Geomancy and Symbolism.* Bar Hill, England: Fenris-Wolf, 1984.

———. *Masterworks: Arts and Crafts of Traditional Buildings in Northern Europe.* Wymeswold, England: Heart of Albion Press, 2002.

———. *Natural Magic.* Earl Shilton, England: Lear Books, 2005.

———. *Natural Measure.* Bar Hill, England: Fenris-Wolf, 1984.

———. *Ogham and Coelbren*: *Keys to the Celtic Mysteries.* Chieveley, England: Capall Bann Publishing, 2000.

———. *On Building in the European Tradition.* Cambridge: Library of the European Tradition, 2000.

———. *On the European Tradition.* Cambridge: Library of the European Tradition, 2000.

———. *Pargetting in Eastern England.* Cambridge: Library of the European Tradition, 2000.

———. *Primal Signs.* Bar Hill, England: Fenris-Wolf, 2007.

———. "The Religion of Northern Europe." In *The Times World Religions,* edited by Martin Palmer, 44–51. London: Times Books, 2002.

———. *Rune Magic.* London: The Aquarian Press, 1992.

———. *Runic Astrology.* Wellingborough, England: Aquarian, 1980.

———. *The Sacred World of the Celts.* London: Thorsons, 1997.

———. *The Secret Lore of Runes and Other Ancient Alphabets.* London: Rider, 1991.

———. *Secret Signs, Symbols and Sigils.* Chieveley, England: Capall Bann Publishing, 1996.

———. *Skulls, Cats and Witch Bottles.* Bar Hill, England: Fenris-Wolf, 1986.

———. *Traditional Board Games of Northern Europe.* Bar Hill, England: Fenris-Wolf, 1988.

———. *Wayland's House.* Cambridge: Cambridge University Press, 1993.

Pennick, Nigel, and Helen Field. *The God Year.* Chieveley, England: Capall Bann Publishing, 1998.

———. *The Goddess Year.* Chieveley, England: Capall Bann Publishing, 1996.

———. *Muses and Fates.* Milverton, England: Penrose, 2004.

Penty, Arthur. *The Restoration of the Gild System.* London: S. Sonnenschein and Company, 1906.

Philippson, Ernst Alfred. *Germanisches Heidentum bei den Angelsachsen.* Leipzig, Germany: Tauchnitz, 1929.

Plennydd. *Barddas: or, a Collection of Original Documents, Illustrative of the Theology, Wisdom, and Usages of The Bardo-Druidic System of the Isle of Britain.* Translated by Ab Ithel (Rev. J. Williams). Llandovery, Wales: The Welch Manuscript Society, 1867.

Puhvel, Jaan. *Myth and Law among the Indo-Europeans*. Berkeley: University of California Press, 1970.

Pushong, Carlyle. *Rune Magic*. London: Regency Press, 1978.

Rackham, Oliver. *The History of the Countryside*. London: J. M. Dent, 1986.

Rees, Alwyn, and Brinley Rees. *Celtic Heritage: Ancient Tradition in Ireland and Wales*. London: Thames & Hudson, 1961.

Reuter, Otto Sigfrid. *Skylore of the North*. Translated by Michael Behrend. Bar Hill, England: Fenris-Wolf, 1985.

Ridley, Nancy. *Portrait of Northumberland*. London: Robert Hale & Company, 1970.

Roberts, Anthony. *Geomancy: A Synthonal Re-appraisal*. Westhay, England: Zodiac House, 1981.

Rowley, Sue, ed. *Tradition and Innovation*. Winchester, England: Telos, 1999.

Sartre, Jean-Paul. *The Psychology of Imagination*. London: Methuen, 1940.

Schuré, Édouard. *Les grands initiés: Esquisse de l'histoire secrète des religions*. Paris: Perrin, 1889.

Schutte, Gudmund. *Dänisches Heidentum*. Heidelberg, Germany: C. Winter, 1923.

Schwedt, Herbert, Elke Schwedt, and Martin Blümke. *Masken und Maskenschnitzer der schwäbisch alemannischen Fasnacht*. Stuttgart: Kommissionsverlag Konrad Theiss, 1984.

Scott, Sir Walter. *Minstrelsy of the Scottish Border*. Edinburgh: James Ballantyne, 1801.

Screeton, Paul. *The Lambton Worm and Other Northumbrian Dragon Legends*. London: Zodiac House, 1978.

Sheffield, John. *The Original Robin Hood*. Nottingham, England: Sheffield & Broad, 1982.

Sikes, Wirt. *British Goblins: The Realm of the Faerie*. London: Sampson Low, Marston, Searle & Rivington, 1880.

Smith, Alan. *Sixty Saxon Saints*. Hockwold-cum-Wilton, England: Anglo-Saxon Books, 1994.

Smith, Gavin. "Recovering the Lost Religious Place-Names of England." *At the Edge*, September 1996, 12–19.

Smith, Toulmin. *English Guilds*. London: Oxford University Press, 1870.

Sommer, Robert. *The Mind's Eye: Imagery in Everyday Life*. New York: Delacorte Press, 1978.

Spence, Lewis. *British Fairy Origins*. London: Watts & Company, 1946.

———. *The Minor Traditions of British Mythology.* London: Rider and Company, 1948.

———. *Myth and Ritual in Dance, Game and Rhyme.* London: Watts & Company, 1947.

Starmore, Alice, and Anne Matheson. *Knitting from the British Islands.* London: Book Club Associates, 1983.

Stenton, Frank. *Anglo-Saxon England.* Oxford: Oxford University Press, 1971.

Tabor, Raymond. *Traditional Woodland Crafts.* London: Batsford Ltd., 1994.

Taylor, Charles. *The Malaise of Modernity.* Toronto, Ont.: Anansi, 1991.

Thomas, Val. *A Witch's Kitchen.* Chieveley, England: Capall Bann Publishing, 2002.

Thorsson, Edred. *Futhark: A Handbook of Rune Magic.* York Beach, England: Red Wheel Weiser, 1987.

———. *Green Runa.* Austin, Tex.: Rûna-Raven, 1993.

Tiller, Alexander. *Yule and Christmas.* London: D. Nutt, 1899.

Tolkien, J. R. R. *Tree and Leaf.* London: George Allen & Unwin, Ltd., 1964.

Tongue, Ruth L. *Forgotten Folk-Tales of the English Counties.* London: Routledge & Kegan Paul, 1970.

Toutain, Jules. *Les cultes païens dans l'Empire Romaine.* Paris: Ernest Leroux, 1911.

Trinkūnas, Jonas, ed. *Of Gods and Holidays: The Baltic Heritage.* Vilnius, Lithuania: Tvermé, 1999.

Turner, Walter James, ed. *British Craftsmanship.* London: Collins, 1948.

Von Zaborsky, Oskar. *Urväter-Erbe in Deutscher Volkskunst.* Leipzig, Germany: Koehler und Amelang, 1936.

Walenkamp, H. J. M. "Voor-historische wijsheid." *Architectura* 12 (1904): 333–36, 376–85; *Architectura* 13 (1905): 185–88.

Weil, Stephen E. *Rethinking the Museum.* Washington, D.C. & London: Smithsonian Institution Press, 1990.

Welch, Martin. *Anglo-Saxon England.* London: Batsford Ltd., 1982.

West, Trudy. *The Timber-Frame House in England.* Newton Abbot, England: David & Charles, 1980.

Wikander, Stig. *Der arische Männerbund.* Lund, Sweden: Ohlsson, 1938.

Williamson, George C. *Curious Survivals.* London: Herbert Jenkins, 1925.

Wilson, Joe. *Tyneside Songs and Drolleries.* Newcastle-on-Tyne, England: Thomas & George Allan, 1891.

Winterbotham, J. J. *Hackness in the Middle Ages.* Hackness, England: Hackness Press, 1985.

Wirth, Hermann. *Die Heilige Urschrift der Menschheit.* 9 vols. Leipzig, Germany: Koehler & Amelang, 1934.

Wood-Martin, William Gregory. *Traces of the Elder Faiths of Ireland.* London: Longmans, Green, & Company, 1902.

Wright, Elizabeth Mary. *Rustic Speech and Folk-Lore.* Oxford: Oxford University Press, 1913.

Wymer, Norman. *English Country Crafts: A Survey from Their Origins to the Present Day.* London: B. T. Batsford Ltd., 1946.

Young, Robert. *Timothy Hackworth and the Locomotive.* Shildon, England: The Locomotive Publishing Company, Ltd., 1923.

Zeller, Otto. *Der Ursprung der Buchstabenschrift und das Runenalphabet.* Osnabrück, Germany: Biblio-Verlag, 1977.

INDEX

Page numbers in *italics* indicate illustrations.